Eat Well Live Well

READER'S DIGEST

Pies, Tarts & Puddings

Eat Well Live Well

READER'S DIGEST

Pies, Tarts
& Puddings

Reader's
Digest

Published by The Reader's Digest Association Limited
London • New York • Sydney • Montreal

PIES, TARTS AND PUDDINGS is part of a series of cookery books called EAT WELL LIVE WELL and was created by Amazon Publishing Limited.

Series Editor *Norma MacMillan*
Volume Editor *Maggie Pannell*
Art Director *Ruth Prentice*
Photographic Direction *Ruth Prentice, Alison Shackleton*
DTP *Claire Graham*
Editorial Assistant *Elizabeth Woodland*
Nutritionist *Jane Griffin, BSc (Nutri.), SRD*

CONTRIBUTORS
Writers *Catherine Atkinson, Sara Buenfeld, Linda Collister, Christine France, Angela Nilsen, Maggie Pannell, Anne Sheasby, Susanna Tee*
Recipe Testers *Catherine Atkinson, Juliet Barker, Bridget Jones, Jane Middleton, Maggie Pannell, Susanna Tee*
Photographers *Martin Brigdale, Gus Filgate, William Lingwood*
Stylist *Helen Trent*
Home Economists *Julz Beresford, Lucy McKelvie, Bridget Sargeson, Linda Tubby, Sunil Vijayakar*

FOR READER'S DIGEST
Project Editor *Rachel Warren Chadd*
Project Art Editor *Louise Turpin*
Pre-press Accounts Manager *Penny Grose*

READER'S DIGEST GENERAL BOOKS
Editorial Director *Cortina Butler*
Art Director *Nick Clark*
Series Editor *Christine Noble*

ISBN 0 276 42479 4

First Edition Copyright © 2002
The Reader's Digest Association Limited
11 Westferry Circus, Canary Wharf, London E14 4HE
www.readersdigest.co.uk

Copyright © 2002 Reader's Digest Association Far East Limited
Philippines copyright © 2002 Reader's Digest Association Far East Limited

We are committed to both the quality of our products and the service we provide to our customers. We value your comments, so please feel free to contact us on 08705 113366, or via our website at www.readersdigest.co.uk
If you have any comments about the content of our books, you can contact us at: gbeditorial@readersdigest.co.uk

Notes for the reader
• Use all metric or all imperial measures when preparing a recipe, as the two sets of measurements are not exact equivalents.
• Recipes were tested using metric measures and conventional (not fan-assisted) ovens. Medium eggs were used, unless otherwise specified.
• Can sizes are approximate, as weights can vary slightly according to the manufacturer.
• Preparation and cooking times are only intended as a guide.

The nutritional information in this book is for reference only. The editors urge anyone with continuing medical problems or symptoms to consult a doctor.

Contents

56
Simple Family Meals

82
Savoury Dishes for Entertaining

104
Sweet Pies and Tarts

128
Sweet Puddings

Eating well to live well

Eating a healthy diet can help you look good, feel great and have lots of energy. Nutrition fads come and go, but the simple keys to eating well remain the same: enjoy a variety of food – no single food contains all the vitamins, minerals, fibre and other essential components you need for health and vitality – and get the balance right by looking at the proportions of the different foods you eat. Add some regular exercise too – at least 30 minutes a day, 3 times a week – and you'll be helping yourself to live well and make the most of your true potential.

Getting it into proportion

Current guidelines are that most people in the UK should eat more starchy foods, more fruit and vegetables, and less fat, meat products and sugary foods. It is almost impossible to give exact amounts that you should eat, as every single person's requirements vary, depending on size, age and the amount of energy expended during the day. However, nutrition experts have suggested an ideal balance of the different foods that provide us with energy (calories) and the nutrients needed for health. The number of daily portions of each of the food groups will vary from person to person – for example, an active teenager might need to eat up to 14 portions of starchy carbohydrates every day, whereas a sedentary adult would only require 6 or 7 portions – but the proportions of the food groups in relation to each other should ideally stay the same.

More detailed explanations of food groups and nutritional terms can be found on pages 156–158, together with brief guidelines on amounts which can be used in conjunction with the nutritional analyses of the recipes. A simple way to get the balance right, however, is to imagine a daily 'plate' divided into the different food groups. On the imaginary 'plate', starchy carbohydrates fill at least one-third of the space, thus constituting the main part of your meals. Fruit and vegetables fill the same amount of space. The remaining third of the 'plate' is divided mainly between protein foods and dairy foods, with just a little space allowed for foods containing fat and sugar. These are the proportions to aim for.

It isn't essential to eat the ideal proportions on the 'plate' at every meal, or even every day – balancing them over a week or two is just as good. The healthiest diet for you and your family is one that is generally balanced and sustainable in the long term.

Our daily plate
Starchy carbohydrate foods: eat 6–14 portions a day

At least 50% of the calories in a healthy diet should come from carbohydrates, and most of that from starchy foods – bread, potatoes and other starchy vegetables, pasta, rice and cereals. For most people in the UK this means doubling current intake. Starchy carbohydrates are the best foods for energy. They also provide protein and essential vitamins and minerals, particularly those from the B group. Eat a variety of starchy foods, choosing wholemeal or wholegrain types whenever possible, because the fibre they contain helps to prevent constipation, bowel disease, heart disease and other health problems.

What is a portion of starchy foods?

Some examples are: 3 tbsp breakfast cereal • 2 tbsp muesli • 1 slice of bread or toast • 1 bread roll, bap or bun • 1 small pitta bread, naan bread or chapatti • 3 crackers or crispbreads • 1 medium-sized potato • 1 medium-sized plantain or small sweet potato • 2 heaped tbsp boiled rice • 2 heaped tbsp boiled pasta.

Fruit and vegetables: eat at least 5 portions a day

Nutrition experts are unanimous that we would all benefit from eating more fruit and vegetables each day – a total of at least 400 g (14 oz) of fruit and vegetables (edible part) is the target. Fruit and vegetables provide vitamin C for immunity and healing, and other 'antioxidant' vitamins and minerals for protection against cardiovascular disease and cancer. They also offer several 'phytochemicals' that help protect against cancer, and B vitamins, especially folate, which is important for women planning a pregnancy, to prevent birth defects. All of these, plus other nutrients, work together to boost well-being.

Antioxidant nutrients (e.g. vitamins C and beta-carotene, which are mainly derived from fruit and vegetables) and vitamin E help to prevent harmful free radicals in the body initiating or accelerating cancer, heart disease, cataracts, arthritis, general ageing, sun damage to skin, and damage to sperm. Free radicals occur naturally as a by-product of normal cell function, but are also caused by pollutants such as tobacco smoke and over-exposure to sunlight.

What is a portion of fruit or vegetables?

Some examples are: 1 medium-sized portion of vegetables or salad • 1 medium-sized piece of fresh fruit • 6 tbsp (about 140 g/5 oz) stewed or canned fruit • 1 small glass (100 ml/3½ fl oz) fruit juice.

Dairy foods: eat 2–3 portions a day

Dairy foods, such as milk, cheese, yogurt and fromage frais, are the best source of calcium for strong bones and teeth, and important for the nervous system. They also provide some protein for growth and repair, vitamin B_{12}, and vitamin A for healthy eyes. They are particularly valuable foods for young children, who need full-fat versions at least up to age 2. Dairy foods are also especially important for adolescent girls to prevent the development of osteoporosis later in life, and for women throughout life generally.

To limit fat intake, wherever possible adults should choose lower-fat dairy foods, such as semi-skimmed milk and low-fat yogurt.

What is a portion of dairy foods?

Some examples are: 1 medium-sized glass (200 ml/7 fl oz) milk • 1 matchbox-sized piece (40 g/1½ oz) Cheddar cheese • 1 small pot of yogurt • 125 g (4½ oz) cottage cheese or fromage frais.

Protein foods: eat 2–4 portions a day

Lean meat, fish, eggs and vegetarian alternatives provide protein for growth and cell repair, as well as iron to prevent anaemia. Meat also provides B vitamins for healthy nerves and digestion, especially vitamin B_{12}, and zinc for growth and healthy bones and skin. Only moderate amounts of these protein-rich foods are required. An adult woman needs about 45 g of protein a day and an adult man 55 g, which constitutes about 11% of a day's calories. This is less than the current average intake. For optimum health, we need to eat some protein every day.

What is a portion of protein-rich food?

Some examples are: 3 slices (85–100 g/3–3½ oz) of roast beef, pork, ham, lamb or chicken • about 100 g (3½ oz) grilled offal • 115–140 g (4–5 oz) cooked fillet of white or oily fish (not fried in batter) • 3 fish fingers • 2 eggs (up to 7 a week) • about 140 g/5 oz baked beans • 60 g (2¼ oz) nuts, peanut butter or other nut products.

Foods containing fat: 1–5 portions a day

Unlike fruit, vegetables and starchy carbohydrates, which can be eaten in abundance, fatty foods should not exceed 33% of the day's calories in a balanced diet, and only 10% of this should be from saturated fat. This quantity of fat may seem a lot, but it isn't – fat contains more than twice as many calories per gram as either carbohydrate or protein.

Overconsumption of fat is a major cause of weight and health problems. A healthy diet must contain a certain amount of fat to provide fat-soluble vitamins and essential fatty acids, needed for the development and function of the brain, eyes and nervous system, but we only need a small amount each day – just 25 g is required, which is much less than we consume in our Western diet. The current recommendations from the Department of Health are a maximum of 71 g fat (of this, 21.5 g saturated) for women each day and 93.5 g fat (28.5 g saturated) for men. The best sources of the essential fatty acids are natural fish oils and pure vegetable oils.

What is a portion of fatty foods?

Some examples are: 1 tsp butter or margarine • 2 tsp low-fat spread • 1 tsp cooking oil • 1 tbsp mayonnaise or vinaigrette (salad dressing) • 1 tbsp cream • 1 individual packet of crisps.

Foods containing sugar: 0–2 portions a day

Although many foods naturally contain sugars (e.g. fruit contains fructose, milk lactose), health experts recommend that we limit 'added' sugars. Added sugars, such as table sugar, provide only calories – they contain no vitamins, minerals or fibre to contribute to health, and it is not necessary to eat them at all. But, as the old adage goes, 'a little of what you fancy does you good' and sugar is no exception. Denial of foods, or using them as rewards or punishment, is not a healthy attitude to eating, and can lead to cravings, binges and yo-yo dieting. Sweet foods are a pleasurable part of a well-balanced diet, but added sugars should account for no more than 11% of the total daily carbohydrate intake.

In assessing how much sugar you consume, don't forget that it is a major ingredient of many processed and ready-prepared foods.

What is a portion of sugary foods?

Some examples are: 3 tsp sugar • 1 heaped tsp jam or honey • 2 biscuits • half a slice of cake • 1 doughnut • 1 Danish pastry • 1 small bar of chocolate • 1 small tube or bag of sweets.

Too salty

Salt (sodium chloride) is essential for a variety of body functions, but we tend to eat too much through consumption of salty processed foods, 'fast' foods and ready-prepared foods, and by adding salt in cooking and at the table. The end result can be rising blood pressure as we get older, which puts us at higher risk of heart disease and stroke. Eating more vegetables and fruit increases potassium intake, which can help to counteract the damaging effects of salt.

Alcohol in a healthy diet

In recent research, moderate drinking of alcohol has been linked with a reduced risk of heart disease and stroke among men and women over 45. However, because of other risks associated with alcohol, particularly in excessive quantities, no doctor would recommend taking up drinking if you are teetotal. The healthiest pattern of drinking is to enjoy small amounts of alcohol with food, to have alcohol-free days and always to avoid getting drunk. A well-balanced diet is vital because nutrients from food (vitamins and minerals) are needed to detoxify the alcohol.

Water – the best choice

Drinking plenty of non-alcoholic liquid each day is an often overlooked part of a well-balanced diet. A minimum of 8 glasses (which is about 2 litres/3½ pints) is the ideal. If possible, these should not all be tea or coffee, as these are stimulants and diuretics, which cause the body to lose liquids, taking with them water-soluble vitamins. Water is the best choice. Other good choices are fruit or herb teas or tisanes, fruit juices – diluted with water, if preferred – or semi-skimmed milk (full-fat milk for very young children). Fizzy sugary or acidic drinks such as cola are more likely to damage tooth enamel than other drinks.

As a guide to the vitamin and mineral content of foods and recipes in the book, we have used the following terms and symbols, based on the percentage of the daily RNI provided by one serving for the average adult man or woman aged 19–49 years (see also pages 156–158):

✓✓✓   *or* excellent   at least 50% (half)

✓✓   *or* good   25–50% (one-quarter to one-half)

✓   *or* useful   10–25% (one-tenth to one-quarter)

Note that recipes contribute other nutrients, but the analyses only include those that provide at least 10% RNI per portion. Vitamins and minerals where deficiencies are rare are not included.

Ⓥ denotes that a recipe is suitable for vegetarians.

Wonderful Pies, Tarts and Puddings

A wide choice, both sweet and savoury

The cook who brings a pastry dish or pudding to the table will always be greeted with delight. There is something about these comforting dishes that whets the appetite and makes mealtimes so enjoyable. They can fit perfectly into a healthy diet too, because they incorporate such a wide variety of nutrient-rich ingredients, from protein foods, dairy products, grains and other starchy carbohydrates, to nuts and seeds, and fruit and vegetables. You'll be inspired to create starters, snacks, main dishes and desserts that are both nutritious and delicious.

Healthy pies, tarts and puddings

Fillings wrapped in or topped with pastry, and sweet and savoury puddings may not spring to mind as being the healthiest of dishes, but in fact pies, tarts and puddings can be very nutritious and fit well into healthy eating guidelines. With such a wide variety of appetising recipes, friends and family will be able to tuck in with relish.

Food that really satisfies

Pies, tarts and puddings have been popular since medieval times. Like many traditional dishes, they were developed to meet both practical and nutritional needs, as well as to celebrate special occasions. The pie – a filling encased in an edible crust – was the original convenience food, easy to transport and eat without cutlery. And puddings, both sweet and savoury, were satisfying, warming body and soul. The modern versions show that these homely dishes still have plenty to offer, and can be enjoyed as part of a healthy diet.

Pies to please

A pie consists of a sweet or savoury filling covered with a crust or with a crust both on top and at the bottom. The possibilities for tasty fillings are almost endless. And the choice of crust can be deliciously varied, from pastry, bread and scone dough to polenta, rice, tortillas, sliced or cubed bread, and mashed potatoes and other vegetables. Pies can be made in many shapes and sizes, and can be finished with a glaze, a sprinkle of nuts or cheese, or a pastry decoration.

Pies can be plain and simple, making the most of seasonal produce and turning everyday ingredients into tasty dishes for the family, or more exotic and adventurous ones for a special occasion. And from the point of view of healthy eating, one of the merits of a pie is that a nourishing combination of ingredients can be cooked together in their own juices, retaining maximum flavour and goodness.

Tempting tarts

A tart is usually understood to be an open case filled with a sweet or savoury mixture. It may also be called a quiche, which is traditionally filled with a bacon and Gruyère cheese custard, or a flan. Small individual tarts are usually called tartlets.

The fat issue

Many pies and tarts are made with pastry, which is basically a combination of fat and flour bound with water or other liquid to make a dough. It is the fat that provides texture and flavour. Certain pastries, such as puff and flaky, contain a high proportion of fat to flour and cannot be made successfully by altering the balance of ingredients. Others, such as filo and scone pastry, contain very little fat. Shortcrust pastry, which is the most widely used, can be enjoyed in a healthy diet, but to keep the total fat content down it is best to roll out the pastry thinly and to use it only as a single crust, either as a container for the filling or covering it. Shortcrust can also be made successfully with unsaturated fats such as olive or sunflower oil, rather than butter. With a filling that includes a variety of lean and nutritious ingredients, a pie or tart can make a tasty contribution to healthy family eating or be a special meal for guests.

Tart cases can be made from pastry – most commonly shortcrust or crisp and flaky filo – or from other mixtures such as polenta, yeasted bread dough, bread slices or biscuit crumbs.

Comforting puddings

The word pudding is used to describe a number of different kinds of dishes. Thus a pudding can be a savoury recipe, usually served hot and often made in a pudding basin or other mould, or it can be a sweet dish served at the end of a meal. Sweet puddings may be hot or cold, although cold sweet dishes are often called desserts.

The range of sweet and savoury puddings is wide, from Yorkshire puddings, rice puddings, and sponge puddings to classic family favourites such as crumbles and custards.

► Use deliciously crisp, low-fat filo pastry for Oriental crab, corn and asparagus tartlets (see Some more ideas, page 35)

▼ Try Spiced lamb pie, made with lean lamb and lots of nutritious vegetables and covered with a coriander mash (see Some more ideas, page 87)

▲ Make an apple and blackberry pie full of juicy, healthy fruit and topped with a shortcrust pastry lid (see Some more ideas, page 126)

◄ For a vitamin-C boost, layer fresh raspberries with crunchy amaretti and a creamy yogurt custard (see Some more ideas, page 133)

What pies, tarts and puddings have to offer

With such a wonderful variety of pie, tart and pudding recipes, using ingredients from all the different food groups, it is possible to benefit from just about every nutrient needed for good health and wellbeing.

Dairy foods

Milk, yogurt and cream enrich and moisten puddings and fillings for pies and tarts, while cheeses add flavour. Dairy foods are an excellent source of calcium and phosphorus, both needed for strong teeth and bones. Dairy foods also provide protein, other minerals and a variety of vitamins, including A, B-group and D. Full-fat dairy products can be high in saturated fat, but there are many lower-fat versions that work well in cooking. You can also mix high and lower-fat dairy ingredients or, in the case of cheese, choose those strong in flavour so less is needed for maximum taste impact.

Eggs

Eggs, which add flavour, colour and lightness of texture to many puddings and to pie and tart fillings, are nutrient-rich, providing high-quality protein, useful amounts of vitamins A, B_2, B_{12}, E and niacin, and plenty of minerals.

Fats

Fats help to provide taste and texture in pastry and in fillings for pies, tarts and puddings, making them satisfying to eat, as well as improving their keeping qualities. Fats provide fat-soluble vitamins as well as the essential fatty acids, omega-3 and omega-6. Butter, a pure natural fat, is a particularly good source of vitamins A and D, while oils pressed from fruit, vegetables, nuts and seeds contain beneficial phytochemicals and other nutrients such as the antioxidant vitamin E, which can help to prevent heart disease. Although healthy eating guidelines recommend cutting down on fat intake, particularly the saturated type, some fat is necessary for good health and for good eating.

Flour

The flours used for making pastry, bread doughs, sponges and scones consist mainly of valuable starchy carbohydrate. Flour can also be a good low-fat source of vegetable protein, and of B vitamins, minerals and dietary fibre.

Fruit and vegetables

Including vegetables in savoury pie fillings and puddings, and fruit in sweet pies and puddings, boosts their nutritional content, and is an easy way to help meet the 5-a-day target. Whether fresh, frozen, dried or canned, fruit and vegetables are an important part of a healthy diet, providing a range of valuable minerals, vitamins and other beneficial compounds as well as dietary fibre, essential for a healthy digestion. Some vegetables also supply starchy carbohydrate.

Meat, poultry and fish

Protein foods such as meat, poultry and fish turn savoury pies and puddings into satisfying main dishes. Apart from supplying excellent amounts of high-quality protein, they offer many other nutrients. Red meat is a particularly rich source of zinc, several B-group vitamins (especially vitamin B_{12}, which is principally found in animal foods) and iron. Poultry supplies B vitamins and many essential minerals including iron and zinc. Fish and other seafood provide important minerals such as the powerful antioxidant selenium and iodine. Oily fish also supplies the heart-healthy omega-3 fatty acids.

► Fruit and vegetables are the best food sources of valuable antioxidants such as vitamin C and beta-carotene, and also offer disease-fighting phytochemicals

▼ Lean meat and skinless poultry are first-class protein foods and also provide iron and zinc

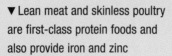

▲ Fish is low in saturated fat, but often high in other beneficial fats, and shellfish is the most reliable natural source of iodine

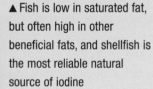

◄ Pulses and grains supply starchy carbohydrates, the foundation of a healthy, well-balanced diet

Nuts and seeds

Nuts and seeds add crunchy texture to pastries as well as to fillings for pies, tarts and puddings. They also contribute protein (a good source for vegetarians), vitamins, minerals and fibre. Nuts and seeds are high in fat, but (with the exception of coconut) this is mostly in the form of the healthier monounsaturated and polyunsaturated fats.

Pulses

Pulses can add important nutrients to savoury pies and puddings, being good sources of vegetable protein and starchy carbohydrate. They also supply B vitamins (including folate), iron, zinc and dietary fibre. Soya beans are especially nourishing, in that they provide high-quality protein, with all 8 amino acids, just like meat, as well as omega-3 fatty acids, most of the B vitamins, vitamin E and a wide range of minerals. Soya products such as tofu also make a superb nutritional contribution to a pie filling.

Rice and other grains

Grains are the basis of wonderful puddings, both sweet and savoury, and add substance to fillings for pies and tarts. In addition to starchy carbohydrate, they offer some protein, several of the B vitamins, many minerals and dietary fibre. Wholegrains (those which retain the bran and germ) are the most nutritious choice. Rice and grains such as buckwheat, maize, millet and quinoa are gluten-free and so useful for those who suffer from coeliac disease.

Pastry variety

Pastry can be wonderfully varied. By using different fats and flours, changing their proportion to each other and how they're combined, or by adding other ingredients, you can create a range of differently textured and flavoured crusts for pies and tarts that will perfectly complement both sweet and savoury fillings.

Healthy pastry

You may be surprised to see the variety of pastries that can be enjoyed as part of a healthy, well-balanced diet, even those pastries thought of as very high in fat.

Choux pastry Although called a pastry, choux is actually a smooth paste. It is made by melting fat with water and then beating in flour and eggs. It is piped or spooned into shape – for profiteroles, éclairs and so on – and then baked to puff it up. The air trapped inside forms a hollow that can be filled with delicious sweet or savoury mixtures.

Filo pastry The wafer-thin sheets of this low-fat pastry (also called strudel pastry) are brushed sparingly with melted butter or oil and then layered up, to be wrapped, rolled or folded around a sweet or savoury filling, used for delicate pastry cases or scrunched over the top of a pie. During baking the pastry becomes crisp and golden brown. While filo can be made at home, it is labour-intensive, so most cooks prefer to use good-quality chilled or frozen filo.

Hot-water crust This is made with just a small amount of fat (traditionally lard), which is melted with boiling water and then mixed with flour to produce a stiff dough. It needs to be shaped while still warm. It is the classic pastry for 'raised' pies, as it bakes into a firm crust, but also makes a good lower-fat topping for a savoury meat pie.

Scone pastry With a texture that is like a cross between a cake and pastry, scone pastry makes an excellent tart case or top crust for a pie, either sweet or savoury. It is lower in fat than shortcrust, but made in the same way – by rubbing fat into flour and binding with liquid, usually milk. A beaten egg can replace part of the milk for extra nutritional value, and sugar, grated cheese, herbs or spices can be added for flavour.

Suetcrust Quick and easy suetcrust is made with shredded suet and self-raising flour (or plain flour with baking powder). Fresh breadcrumbs can replace part of the flour for a lighter texture, and flavourings such as herbs, grated cheese or nuts can be added for extra taste. Suetcrust is used for pies and for puddings, both sweet and savoury, and is traditionally steamed for a moist texture, although it can also be baked. It should be cooked straight away, as the raising agent in the flour will have started to work as soon as the liquid for binding was added.

Shortcrust pastry The most popular and versatile of pastries, with a delightfully crumbly texture, shortcrust is used for all kinds of sweet and savoury pies and tarts. The fat is usually a hard one such as butter, although oil can be substituted, and it is made by the rubbing-in method. Many other ingredients, such as eggs, oats, sugar, nuts, cheese, citrus zest and spices, can be added to provide exciting flavour variations and additional nutrients. You can also make a lower-fat yeasted version, which has a light 'bready' texture.

Fat contents of different pastries

(based on 100 g/3½ oz uncooked weight of the basic pastry doughs on pages 22–24, and bought filo pastry)

	total fat (g)	saturated fat (g)
filo	4.1	
scone	8.5	5.3
potato	9.9	6.4
choux	14.7	8.4
hot-water crust	16.5	6.6
shortcrust, sweet	22.8	14.0
suetcrust	22.9	12.9
shortcrust, savoury	23.9	15.6

wonderful pies, tarts and puddings

choux pastry

filo pastry

hot-water crust

scone pastry

suetcrust

shortcrust pastry

Ingredients for good pastry

Making the right choice of ingredients is all important for achieving perfect results, and it is also the key to making the healthiest and most nutritious pastry.

Flour

Plain flour is best for most pastries, the exceptions being suetcrust and scone pastry, where a raising agent is needed to produce their characteristic finish. For these, self-raising flour (or plain flour with baking powder) is used. Some cooks also like to use self-raising flour for shortcrust pastry, for a crumblier, more cake-like texture. Strong (bread) flour is unsuitable for short pastries, as the results would be tough, but it can be used for choux pastry and for yeasted pastries.

Both white and wholemeal flours can be used for making pastry. Wholemeal flour contains the whole of the grain and therefore retains most of its nutrients, which means it has more vitamins, minerals, fibre and protein than white flour. Pastries made with wholemeal flour alone have an excellent, almost nutty flavour but a heavier texture. A good compromise is to use half white and half wholemeal flour. In addition, you can use brown flour (also called wheatmeal) or Granary flour.

Flour should be sifted to incorporate air and to mix it with other dry ingredients such as raising agents, salt and spices. After sifting wholemeal flour, tip in the bran left in the sieve.

For light-textured pastry, always sift the flour to help to aerate it

Fat

Butter, lard and hard margarines are the fats generally chosen for making pastry, with shredded suet used for suetcrust. Butter gives a lovely short, crumbly texture and the best flavour of all the fats. Lard, which is purified and clarified pork fat, is mild in flavour and gives a good tender texture to pastry, while suet, processed from the crisp white fat surrounding lamb's or beef kidneys, gives suetcrust and suet puddings a melting lightness. (Vegetarians may prefer to use vegetable suet, which is produced from hydrogenated vegetable oils.) Margarine has the same characteristics as butter in pastry-making, but lacks the all-important flavour.

Margarine and other fats produced by hydrogenating vegetable oils, which turns them from liquids into solid fat, contain a high proportion of trans fatty acids. These fats are now thought to be more harmful to health than saturated fat, in increasing the risk of heart disease. For this reason, and because of its superior flavour, butter is recommended for most of the pastries in this book. If you prefer to use margarine, choose one high in monounsaturates, usually made from olive oil, or one labelled 'free from hydrogenated oils' or 'low in trans fats'.

How do fats compare (per 100 g/3½ oz)?				
	total fat*	saturates	polyunsats	monounsats
butter	82 g	54 g	3 g	20 g
margarine (hard)	82 g	31 g	11 g	37 g
suet	87 g	48 g	2 g	32 g
lard	99 g	41 g	10 g	44 g
olive oil	100 g	14 g	11 g	70 g
sunflower oil	100 g	12 g	63 g	20 g

*The total fat figure includes fatty compounds and other fatty acids in addition to saturates and mono and polyunsaturates.

Oils can also be used for making delicious shortcrust pastry. Olive oil has a rich flavour, so is better suited to savoury pies and tarts, whereas oils with a mild flavour, such as sunflower, safflower and corn, can be used for both sweet and savoury shortcrust pastries.

Soft tub margarines and low-fat spreads are not suitable for traditional pastry-making as they have a different composition and a high water content. They should only be used in recipes specially developed for them.

The liquid element

During baking, the liquid in pastry turns to steam, which can help the pastry to rise and to lighten its texture. The amount of liquid given in a recipe can only be approximate as more or less may be needed, depending on the flour used and the humidity in the kitchen. Pastry made with wholemeal flour needs a little more liquid than one made with white flour.

- Egg or egg yolk, often combined with a little milk or water, enriches pastry. It makes shortcrust shorter in texture, with a lovely golden-coloured crust; in choux pastry, beaten egg creates lightness and volume. Egg also provides additional binding and helps to give a sharp edge to a shortcrust tart case.
- Milk will make a slightly softer pastry than egg. Or you can use plain low-fat yogurt for a pleasant tangy flavour.
- Water is the liquid most commonly used for binding pastry ingredients. If it is very cold, it will help to keep the pastry cool while you work with it. Fruit juice is another option.

Why not try fruit juice, such as orange, apple or lemon, instead of water for binding pastry ingredients together? The juice will add a subtle flavour. As with water, add only enough juice to moisten the ingredients so they can be gathered together into a ball

Interesting extras

Lots of other ingredients can be added to pastry to ring the changes with interesting flavours and textures, as well as to help to boost the nutritional value.

- Cheese makes a tasty addition to savoury pastries and is also good for an apple pie. Hard cheeses such as mature Cheddar and Parmesan are high in fat, but you don't need to add very much as they have a strong flavour. Grate the cheese finely and stir in just before adding the liquid. Add a pinch of cayenne pepper or a little dry mustard too, to help to bring out the cheese flavour. Another idea is to replace some of the butter or other fat with reduced-fat soft cheese or a crumbly cheese like feta.
- Citrus zest, particularly lemon and orange zest, adds a delicious flavour to sweet pastries and to some savoury ones. If liked, the fruit's juice can be used in place of some or all of the water to bind the dough together.
- Ground nuts, such as hazelnuts, almonds and walnuts, can be used in short pastries in place of some of the flour, enriching and adding texture.
- Herbs are delicious in pastry for savoury pies and tarts, and give it pretty green specks. Use 1–2 tbsp chopped fresh herbs or 1–2 tsp dried. Good choices include chives, parsley, sage, thyme, coriander, tarragon and basil, depending on the filling.
- Oats and oatmeal can replace some of the flour in short pastry, adding a lovely rough texture and subtle nutty flavour. Oaty shortcrust is good for both sweet and savoury pies and tarts, and works particularly well with fresh and dried fruit, cheese and vegetable fillings.
- Spices of all kinds can be sifted with the flour. Chilli and curry powders are great in pastry for spicy meat or vegetable fillings, and sweet spices such as ground cinnamon, nutmeg, allspice or mixed spice are perfect for fruit pies and tarts. Use 1–2 tsp of the spice, according to the strength required. For an attractive and tasty finish, you can sprinkle seeds such as fennel, cumin or caraway over the top crust of pies before baking.
- Sugar adds sweetness to pastries. Caster sugar is the one most often used, as it has fine grains that dissolve easily. Sifted icing sugar is also suitable.

The art of pastry-making

Master the skills of pastry-making and you'll rapidly gain yourself a reputation for being a brilliant cook! There's nothing particularly difficult to learn, just some basic techniques that, if followed, will guarantee successful results. Don't let lack of time be an excuse for not making your own pastry, as most are really quick and easy.

Rubbing in

This is the method used to combine fat and flour for shortcrust and scone pastries. The fat should be cool, but not straight from the fridge, when it would be very hard and would take longer to rub in.

Use just your fingertips to blend the diced fat with the sifted flour. Lift the mixture from the bowl as you rub in, to incorporate air. When the mixture is in fine crumbs, like breadcrumbs, bind it together with a little cold water (or other liquid). Add the liquid slowly, as too much will result in a sticky dough that will shrink during baking and turn out hard and tough. Conversely, if the dough is too dry, it will crack when rolled out and be difficult to handle, will crumble after baking and be dry to eat.

You can also make rubbed-in pastries very successfully in a food processor fitted with a metal blade or a special pastry-making attachment. In this case, the fat should be very cold and firm, straight from the fridge, and cut into small pieces. Add it to the sifted flour in the processor bowl and mix or pulse for about 3 seconds or until the mixture resembles breadcrumbs. Gradually pour in about two-thirds of the cold liquid through the feed tube, with the motor running, and whizz for a further few seconds, just until a ball of dough is formed. Turn off immediately or the pastry will be over-mixed and difficult to handle. Only add the remaining liquid if the dough doesn't bind together. With a food processor, slightly less liquid is needed as the action of the blades tends to make the dough a little more sticky.

When rubbing in (left), use your fingertips only, to prevent the heat of your hands softening the fat. Add the liquid gradually (above), mixing it in with a table knife. Add just enough liquid to bind the rubbed-in mixture into a dough (right)

► To line a flan tin, drape the rolled-out dough over the tin (near right), gently ease it in (middle right) and then neatly trim off the excess dough (far right)

▼ For baking blind (below), prick the pastry case with a fork, then line with paper and fill with baking beans

Lining a flan tin

When making a tart case, you can use either a metal flan tin, preferably loose-bottomed so it will be easy to remove the baked pastry case, or a flan ring placed on a baking sheet. China flan dishes look attractive, but do not conduct the heat effectively, so the pastry base can turn out a little soggy.

Roll out the pastry dough to a shape about 5 cm (2 in) larger than the flan tin. Lift the dough carefully by draping it over the rolling pin – it's less likely to tear and easier to position this way – and lay it centrally over the tin. Starting from the middle and working out to the sides, carefully ease the dough into the tin without pulling or stretching, then press it gently against the bottom and sides of the tin. If the dough cracks or tears, simply press it back together. When it is neatly lining the tin, fold the excess dough back over the rim of the tin and roll the rolling pin across to trim off the excess. Prick the bottom lightly all over with a fork to release trapped air (this could cause the pastry to rise during baking).

Baking blind

Tart cases are often baked before the filling is added, either partially, just to set and dry the pastry, or completely. To bake unfilled, or 'blind', first line the pastry case with a sheet of greaseproof paper or foil, pressing it neatly into the corners, then weigh the paper down with dried beans or special ceramic baking beans. This will prevent the pastry from rising and losing its shape during baking.

Bake in a preheated hot oven for about 15 minutes, or according to the recipe, then lift out the paper or foil and beans. Return the pastry case to the oven to bake for a further 5 minutes to dry out, or 15 more minutes to cook the pastry case completely (follow individual recipe instructions).

For tartlet cases to be baked blind, it is not necessary to use the paper and beans. Just prick the bottoms well all over with a fork before baking.

Getting ahead

Having pastry on hand is a boon for a busy cook, so why not make a batch when you have some spare time. The rubbed-in mixture can be kept in an airtight container in the fridge for up to 2 weeks, needing only a little liquid to be added to bind it. Pastry dough, wrapped tightly in cling film or greaseproof paper, will keep for 2–3 days in the fridge, or it can be frozen for up to 3 months. Another idea is to freeze pastry cases, in the tin. Bake from frozen, allowing an extra 5–10 minutes, without the paper and beans.

Tips for success

● **Keep everything cool.** Coldness is essential for good pastry and that means keeping the equipment and ingredients cool, as well as your hands. If you have 'hot hands', rinse them under a cold tap to cool them down before starting. In warm weather make your pastry early in the morning while the kitchen is still cool. Once made, shortcrust and scone pastries should be chilled for at least 30 minutes before rolling out. This allows the pastry to

firm up, making it easier to roll. Chilling also removes the elasticity that can cause shrinkage during baking. If time allows, the pastry should also be chilled for 10–15 minutes after it has been rolled. During this time you could make the pie or tart filling.

● **Roll out thinly.** Use the minimum amount of pastry to line a tin or cover a pie. Not only is thinner pastry lighter to eat, but the fat content per serving will be less. When rolling, sprinkle the surface very lightly with flour to prevent the dough from sticking – if too much flour is incorporated into the pastry dough during rolling, the finished texture will be dry and heavy. Roll lightly but firmly in one direction only, then lift the dough, turn and roll again. A marble slab is ideal for rolling out as it helps to keep the pastry cool.

● **Handle with care.** Excessive handling and over-stretching the pastry dough will cause it to shrink on baking, as will adding too much liquid when mixing. So make and roll out the pastry with the minimum of handling, and take care not to stretch it when lining the tin.

● **Prevent soggy pastry.** Always place flan tins on a hot baking sheet in a preheated oven. The baking sheet will help to conduct heat to the base of the pastry case and ensure that it is crisp. Baking blind also helps to prevent soggy pastry. An extra precaution is to brush the bottom of the pastry case with a little beaten egg after removing the beans and paper. When the pastry case is returned to the oven for further baking, the egg will cook and seal the surface. For a top crust pie, let the filling cool before covering with the pastry, and make a small hole in the pastry lid to allow steam from the filling to escape.

Good equipment for healthy baking

Kitchen shops, department stores and large supermarkets now sell a wide range of good-quality tins and baking sheets.

● A heavy rolling pin of a good size will make it easy to roll out pastry thinly and evenly.

● Non-stick tins are ideal for healthy baking as they eliminate the need for greasing with fat. Alternatively, you can line tins or baking sheets with non-stick baking parchment.

● Deep tins allow room for plenty of filling in proportion to the amount of pastry used. It is the filling that provides most of the valuable nutrients in a pie or tart.

● A pastry brush is essential for lightly glazing the tops of pies with milk or beaten egg, and for brushing melted butter or oil sparingly on sheets of filo pastry.

Pie and tart finishes

There are many ways of enhancing the appearance of pies and tarts, making them all the more appetising and good to eat. And some finishes add nutritional benefits too.

● **To 'knock up' the edges of a top crust**, hold a sharp knife horizontally to the side of the pastry edge and make shallow cuts all the way round, while pressing down lightly on the top of the pastry with your other forefinger.

● **To flute or scallop the edge**, press your thumb onto the edge of the crust and, at the same time, draw the back of a knife next to your thumb from the edge towards the centre of the pie. Continue round the pie at 2.5 cm (1 in) intervals.

crimp for a decorative edge

add shapes cut from trimmings

make a lattice topping

glaze a fruit tart with melted jam

- **To crimp the edge**, push your forefinger into the outside of the edge of the crust, then with the forefinger and thumb of your other hand gently pinch the pushed-up pastry together. Continue round the edge of the pie.
- **For a lattice top**, cut the pastry dough into strips and arrange over the filling at right angles across each other. The strips can be interwoven or twisted for a more elaborate effect.
- **Cut leaves or other small shapes** from pastry trimmings and arrange on the top of a pie, sticking them on with a little milk or beaten egg.
- **Brush the pastry with milk or beaten egg** for a crisp, golden finish.
- **Brush the pastry with water** and then sprinkle with poppy, sesame, cumin or fennel seeds, oats, or flaked or chopped nuts.
- **Glaze the filling in a fruit tart.** Warm a little jam, marmalade or redcurrant jelly until melted, then sieve it if necessary before brushing over the fruit. Leave to cool and set.

Working with filo

There are many different brands of filo pastry available, and the size and thickness of the sheets varies. For consistency, all the recipes for filo in this book use authentic Greek pastry, which is available from larger supermarkets. This comes in thin, large sheets measuring about 30 x 50 cm (12 x 20 in). If using smaller sheets, simply increase the number and cut to size following the recipe instructions.

- If using frozen filo, let it thaw for 4–5 hours or overnight in the fridge, or for 2–3 hours at room temperature, before opening the packet. When thawed, unroll and remove as many sheets as needed for the recipe, then re-wrap and return the remainder to the box. It will remain fresh in the fridge for up to 2 days.
- Filo dries out very quickly, so keep the stacked-up sheets covered with cling film or a tea-towel, with a second damp tea-towel laid over the top. Do not allow the damp towel to rest on the pastry as this will make the sheets sticky. Remove the sheets one at a time as they are used, keeping the remainder covered. It doesn't matter if some sheets are torn, as they can be used between whole sheets. If filo pies and tarts are not to be baked immediately, keep them covered with cling film.

Basic pastries

These recipes provide the wrapping or covering for many pies and tarts, both sweet and savoury. You will find them used in recipes in this book. Follow individual recipe instructions for methods of use and baking.

Shortcrust pastry

Makes enough to line a deep 20–23 cm (8–9 in) flan tin or to cover a large pie dish for serving 4–6
170 g (6 oz) plain flour
pinch of salt
85 g (3 oz) cool butter, diced

Preparation time: 10 minutes, plus at least 30 minutes chilling

1 Sift the flour and salt into a large mixing bowl. Add the butter and rub into the flour until the mixture resembles breadcrumbs.
2 Sprinkle with 3 tbsp of cold water and mix in using a round-bladed knife. Add a drop more water only if the dough will not clump together. With your hands, gather together into a firm but pliable dough, handling as little as possible.
3 Wrap the ball of dough in greaseproof paper or cling film and chill for at least 30 minutes before rolling out.

Some more ideas
• For wholemeal shortcrust, use half wholemeal flour and half white flour. A little extra water may be needed.
• Use self-raising flour for a lighter texture.
• Use half lard and half butter for a shorter texture.
• For olive oil shortcrust, replace the butter with 4 tbsp extra virgin olive oil. Add to the flour together with 1 egg beaten with 1 tbsp tepid water. Mix using a fork rather than rubbing in. Add a bit more water if needed. Leave to rest at room temperature for 30 minutes rather than chilling. For a sweet tart, use sunflower or corn oil instead of olive.
• For oatmeal shortcrust, replace 55 g (2 oz) of the flour with rolled oats. Bind with cold water as in the main recipe, or use 1 beaten egg with 1 tbsp water.

• For Parmesan shortcrust, add 25 g (scant 1 oz) finely grated fresh Parmesan cheese after rubbing in the fat.
• For spiced shortcrust, add 1 tsp ground spice to the flour (such as cumin, curry powder, cinnamon or ginger).
• For herbed shortcrust, add 1 tbsp finely chopped fresh herbs or 1 tsp dried herbs to the flour.

Sweet shortcrust pastry

Makes enough to line a shallow 23 cm (9 in) flan tin
115 g (4 oz) plain flour
55 g (2 oz) cool unsalted butter, diced
25 g (scant 1 oz) icing sugar, sifted
1 egg yolk

Preparation time: 10 minutes, plus at least 30 minutes chilling

1 Sift the flour into a mixing bowl. Add the butter and rub in until the mixture resembles fine breadcrumbs. Stir in the sugar.
2 Lightly beat the egg yolk with 1 tbsp cold water. Add to the flour mixture and mix in with a round-bladed knife. Gather together to make a soft dough.
3 Wrap in cling film and chill for at least 30 minutes before rolling out.

Some more ideas
• For sweet almond shortcrust, replace 30 g (1 oz) of the flour with ground almonds (or hazelnuts or walnuts).
• For orange sweet shortcrust, add the finely grated zest of 1 orange (or 1 lemon) with the sugar, and replace the water with orange juice (or lemon juice).
• Add 1 tsp pure vanilla extract to the beaten egg yolk and reduce the amount of water slightly.

wonderful pies, tarts and puddings

Scone pastry

Makes enough to cover a large pie dish for serving 4–6 or to cut out 6 individual large scones

200 g (7 oz) self-raising flour
1 tsp baking powder
pinch of salt
30 g (1 oz) cool butter, diced
100 ml (3½ fl oz) cold semi-skimmed milk

Preparation time: 10 minutes

1 Sift the flour, baking powder and salt into a bowl. Add the butter and rub in until the mixture resembles fine crumbs.
2 Make a well in the centre and add the milk. Mix with a wooden spoon or your fingers to make a fairly soft but not sticky dough, adding a little more milk if necessary.
3 Transfer the dough to a lightly floured surface and knead briefly, then roll out and use as required.

Some more ideas

• Use half self-raising wholemeal flour and half self-raising white flour.
• Replace the milk with 100 g (3 ½ oz) plain low-fat yogurt.
• For herbed scone pastry, add 2 tbsp each chopped fresh chives and parsley and 1 tbsp chopped fresh thyme before mixing in the milk or yogurt.
• For cheese scone pastry, add 25 g (scant 1 oz) finely grated Parmesan or Cheddar cheese.

Choux pastry

Makes enough for a 20 cm (8 in) choux ring or 5–6 choux buns

55 g (2 oz) butter
75 g (2½ oz) plain flour, sifted
2 eggs, beaten with a pinch of salt

Preparation time: 15 minutes

1 Put the butter and 150 ml (5 fl oz) water in a saucepan. Heat gently until the butter has melted, then bring to the boil.
2 As soon as the water boils, remove the pan from the heat and quickly tip in the flour all at once. Beat with a wooden spoon until the ingredients bind together into a dough.
3 Return the pan to a low heat and continue to beat until the dough is a smooth, dry ball in the centre of the pan.
4 Allow to cool for 2–3 minutes, then gradually beat in the eggs to make a smooth, shiny paste. Beat vigorously. Use straight away, as directed in the recipe.

Hot-water crust

Makes enough to cover a 1.2 litre (2 pint) pie dish
115 g (4 oz) plain flour
pinch of salt
30 g (1 oz) lard
1 tbsp semi-skimmed milk

Preparation time: 10 minutes

1 Sift the flour and salt into a mixing bowl. Put the lard, milk and 2 tbsp water into a saucepan and heat gently until melted, then bring to the boil. Pour into the bowl.
2 Mix the liquid into the flour using a wooden spoon, then beat to form a fairly soft dough, adding a few drops of boiling water if the dough is too stiff.
3 Turn onto a lightly floured surface and knead until smooth. Use while still warm, as directed in the recipe. (If not used immediately, keep covered with a cloth or upturned bowl to prevent the dough from cooling and hardening.)

Suetcrust

Makes enough to cover a large pie dish for 4–6 servings
115 g (4 oz) self-raising flour
pinch of salt
55 g (2 oz) shredded beef suet

Preparation time: 5 minutes

1 Sift the flour and salt into a mixing bowl. Stir in the suet.
2 Add 3–4 tbsp cold water and mix to make a firm but soft dough. Knead lightly in the bowl until smooth. Roll out on a floured surface and use immediately, as directed in the recipe.

Some more ideas
• For cheese suetcrust, add 30 g (1 oz) grated mature Cheddar, Parmesan or other hard cheese before mixing in the water.
• For herbed suetcrust, add 1–2 tbsp chopped fresh herbs with the suet.
• For a richer, more nutritious suetcrust, replace the water with 1 beaten egg plus just enough water to bind the dough together.

• For sweet suetcrust, add 1 tsp caster sugar to the flour and omit the salt. Replace the water with semi-skimmed milk.
• For a lighter suetcrust, replace 30 g (1 oz) of the flour with fresh white breadcrumbs.

Potato pastry

Makes enough to cover a large pie dish for 4–6 servings
300 g (10½ oz) potatoes, peeled and cubed
2 tbsp semi-skimmed milk
115 g (4 oz) plain flour
pinch of salt
55 g (2 oz) cool butter, diced

Preparation time: 20 minutes, plus cooling and at least 30 minutes chilling

1 Cook the potatoes in a saucepan of boiling water for 8–10 minutes or until just tender. Drain well, then mash with the milk. Set aside to cool.
2 Sift the flour and salt into a large mixing bowl. Add the butter and rub in until the mixture resembles fine breadcrumbs.
3 Add the mashed potatoes to the rubbed-in mixture and mix together to form a soft dough. Wrap in cling film and chill for at least 30 minutes before rolling out.

Some more ideas
• For a richer colour and flavour, beat 1 egg yolk into the mashed potato.
• For cheesy potato pastry, add 30 g (1 oz) grated mature Cheddar, Parmesan or other hard cheese plus a pinch of mustard powder to the mashed potato before cooling.
• For herbed potato pastry, add 1–2 tbsp chopped fresh herbs, such as basil and tarragon, to the mashed potato.

Alternatives to pastry

There are many foods you can use for pie cases and top crusts other than pastry. They will add further interest and variety to pies and tarts, both sweet and savoury, and they'll supply nutrients vital for good health. In addition, most are lower in fat than pastry. Some of these pastry alternatives will be familiar, but others are a little more unusual. Do try them to make new and exciting dishes.

- **Biscuit crumbs** can be used as the base for sweet and savoury tarts, usually combined with melted fat. For a lower-fat version, simply sprinkle crushed crumbs over a lightly buttered tin. Ginger or oaty biscuits and Italian amaretti work particularly well for sweet tarts, and water biscuits can be used for savoury ones. Another good idea is to combine biscuit crumbs with enough beaten egg white to bind, press over the bottom and sides of a non-stick tin, and bake until set.

- **Bread**, an excellent source of starchy carbohydrate plus many vitamins and minerals, can be sliced, cubed or turned into crumbs for a pie topping, or slices can be rolled out thinly and used to line little tins for savoury tarts. All kinds of bread are suitable, from white and wholemeal to oat, Granary, ciabatta, challah, sourdough, rye and so on.

- **Bread and pizza doughs** make a good low-fat case for a tart. Flavour the dough with a little freshly grated Parmesan cheese, if you like. Good fillings include those ingredients typically suited to pizza toppings, such as tomatoes, mushrooms, olives, anchovies and seafood.

- **Polenta (maize or cornmeal)** is a good gluten-free source of starchy carbohydrates. It can be cooked and left to cool, then rolled out and used to line a flan tin or to make a top crust. Use stock instead of water and add chopped fresh herbs or a little finely grated cheese for extra flavour.

- **Rice**, another gluten-free starchy carbohydrate, makes a delicious tart case. Risotto rice works particularly well as it is creamy when cooked (rice that keeps its grains separate, such as basmati, is not suitable). Let the rice cool, then press into the tin and bake. A beaten egg added to the rice will help to bind the mixture together. Couscous bound with egg is another imaginative possibility.

- **Sponge mixtures** made from a whisked eggs and sugar with flour folded in, are almost fat-free. Bake in a sponge flan tin for a fruit filling.

- **Tortillas and pancakes** make a novel tart case, or they can be layered up with a cooked filling to make a pie. Soft flour tortillas (wraps) and corn tortillas, both good sources of starchy carbohydrates, work well with spicy minced meat or vegetable fillings and make well-balanced pies. Pancakes offer protein and calcium too.

- **Vegetables** such as potatoes, swede, winter squashes, parsnips, carrots and sweet potatoes make delicious and colourful toppings for pies, and add valuable vitamins, minerals and fibre. Some supply starchy carbohydrates too. Use 1 vegetable alone, or combine 2 or more. Mash or roughly crush the vegetables, or slice or cube them. Flavour mash with chopped fresh herbs, pesto, garlic, sun-dried tomatoes, mustard, citrus zest or cheese, or mix with chopped watercress, or steamed shredded greens, cabbage or leeks.

Puddings for all occasions

Traditional British cooking is famous for its wonderful puddings, both savoury and sweet. Those rich with meat and vegetables make substantial and nourishing main dishes, while sweet ones, filled with fresh or dried fruit and nuts, are for many the high point of a meal. Puddings can make a great contribution to a well-balanced diet.

Batter puddings

A simple mixture of eggs, flour and milk can be turned into so many puddings, from pancakes and Yorkshire puddings to toad-in-the-hole and the French classic, clafoutis. The combination of the 3 key ingredients provides useful amounts of protein, starchy carbohydrate and calcium, as well as many other nutrients, making batter puddings very nutritious.

• Use half milk and half water for a lighter result.
• Whisk batters for baked puddings well to incorporate the air needed for a good rise.
• Bake in a tin rather than an ovenproof dish, as metal is a better conductor of heat and will produce a crisper result.
• Serve baked batter puddings immediately, while they are still puffed and risen.

Bread puddings

Bread puddings have long been popular as a good way to use up slightly stale bread, and as an economical and filling sweet course. Today, new bread puddings are being devised, both sweet and savoury, with exciting twists on traditional recipes. The bread can be whatever you fancy – all kinds supply essential starchy carbohydrates.

• Layer slices or cubes of bread with lots of vegetables, then pour over a savoury egg custard and bake.
• Add dried fruits and nuts to sweet bread puddings, or base them on fruited loaves, teabreads or brioche.
• Make a glorious summer pudding, by lining a basin with slices of bread, challah or brioche and filling with soft summer fruits. A variation with autumn fruits is equally good.
• Try a charlotte: line a deep tin with bread, fill with stewed fruit and bake.
• Top a savoury mixture with breadcrumbs tossed with melted butter, oil or grated cheese, then bake or grill until crisp.

Crumbles and cobblers

A crumble is simply a shortcrust pastry mixture, rubbed-in to the 'breadcrumb' stage, that is sprinkled over the top of a fruit, vegetable or other filling and then baked. A cobbler uses scone pastry to cover the filling. For a sweet dish, the crumble mixture or scone dough usually includes a little sugar. With a generous amount of fruit, a sweet crumble or cobbler can be a very healthy and nutritious pudding. Savoury crumbles and cobblers make well-balanced main dishes.

• Add ingredients such as nuts, oats, seeds, muesli, chopped herbs or grated cheese to crumble mixtures and scone doughs, to boost the nutritional value.
• Roll out scone dough and lay it in a sheet over the filling. Or, cut it into shapes, or into strips to be laid as a lattice.

Rice puddings

Although sometimes dismissed as nursery food, rice puddings can have a lot of appeal, particularly the innovative modern versions. And they are full of good things such as eggs, milk and rice, which are very nourishing. Short-grain or pudding rice is generally the best type to use for sweet puddings, as the short, plump grains cook to a creamy consistency. Risotto rice is a good choice for savoury rice puddings.

• Flavour sweet rice puddings with lemon zest, pure vanilla extract, almond essence, bay leaf, saffron, grated nutmeg, cinnamon sticks, cardamom seeds or rosewater.
• Add dried fruits such as cherries, cranberries and blueberries or chopped nuts.
• Pack lots of vegetables into savoury rice puddings and enrich them with grated cheese.
• Stir in some fromage frais or Greek-style yogurt just before serving, to add creaminess without a lot of fat.
• Serve sweet rice puddings with a fruit compote or purée.

◄ Top a cannellini bean and mixed vegetable stew with a cheese and oat crumble mixture (see Some more ideas, page 75) for a nourishing vegetarian main dish

▼ Make a savoury rice pudding by cooking rice in tomato juice and mixing it with antioxidant-rich peppers and tomatoes (see Some more ideas, page 79)

▲ Brown lean and meaty venison sausages in the oven, then surround with a fresh herb-flavoured batter for an unusual toad-in-the-hole (see Some more ideas, page 61)

► Spread slices of fruit loaf with orange marmalade, layer with dried peaches and pour over a brandy custard to make an extra-fruity bread pudding (see Some more ideas, page 130)

Use a big spoon to fold whisked egg whites into the soufflé base

Soufflés

A light, fluffy soufflé can be sweet or savoury, hot or cold, and is quick and easy to make. A hot soufflé is traditionally based on a thick white sauce called a panada, which can be thickened with cornflour for a very low-fat result. Egg yolks are beaten into the panada, and then stiffly whisked egg whites are folded in just before baking. Hot soufflés can be based on a thick purée of fruit or vegetables rather than a panada. Cold soufflés are set with gelatine.

● Whisk egg whites in a clean, dry bowl until they will hold stiff peaks, then fold them immediately into the soufflé base. Stir about one-quarter of the whites in first, to lighten the base, then gently fold in the rest. This will retain the air beaten into the whites.

● Be sure the dish for a hot soufflé is evenly buttered, so the mixture will rise up straight and tall during baking.

● Serve hot soufflés straight from the oven, as they will start to deflate within 1–2 minutes.

Sponge puddings

A whisked sponge, used for Swiss rolls, is a light, almost fatless mixture made by whisking eggs with sugar until they are thick and frothy, and then folding in flour. Melted butter can be added, which will help to keep the sponge moist for longer. Another kind of sponge, used for steamed or baked puddings, is based on a creamed butter and sugar mixture, to which eggs and flour are added. A quick all-in-one version can be made with softened butter, eggs, sugar and self-raising flour, beaten together with an electric mixer.

● For a chocolate sponge, a little of the flour can be replaced with cocoa powder. This adds a rich chocolate flavour without the fat of chocolate.

● Fresh or dried fruit in a sponge pudding adds sweetness, so the amount of sugar can be reduced.

● Use sunflower or other oil instead of butter, for a pudding lower in saturated fat.

Bake fresh plums in a sponge mixture flavoured with ginger (see Some more ideas, page 138) for a zesty, fibre-rich pudding

● When whisking eggs with sugar, if not using an electric mixer, set the bowl over a pan of hot, almost boiling water. This will help the mixture increase in volume.

● For a lighter baked or steamed sponge pudding, replace part of the flour with fresh breadcrumbs.

● Roll the sponge for a Swiss roll while it is warm, otherwise it will crack.

Custards

Egg custards are real comfort food, whether in the form of a pouring sauce or as a sweet or savoury pudding baked in a mould until softly set. Powdered custard mixes are quick and foolproof, but they are made just with cornflour, flavouring and colouring and so do not have the same nutritional benefits as a real egg custard.

● Bake custard puddings gently by setting the mould in a bain-marie (a roasting tin of water). This will protect the custard from overheating, which can spoil its texture.

● Cook custard sauces in a heavy-based saucepan, without letting them boil. If the custard does start to curdle or become lumpy, a quick rescue remedy is to pour it into a blender or food processor, add an ice cube and blend until smooth.

wonderful pies, tarts and puddings

28

Puddings cooked in the steam and heat from boiling liquid have a wonderfully light and moist texture. The true, natural flavours of the ingredients are preserved and, as the pudding doesn't come into direct contact with the liquid, water-soluble vitamins are not lost. You can steam a pudding set on a rack over boiling water in a steamer or immersed in boiling water in a saucepan. Steamed puddings can also be cooked in a pressure cooker or microwave, following the manufacturer's instructions.

● When covering the pudding basin, tie on the foil or greaseproof paper securely with string so the covering cannot slip off. Make a loop with the string to act as a handle so the basin can be lifted out of the steamer or pan (see below).

● Be sure the lid of the steamer or pan fits tightly so that steam cannot escape.

● The water level in a saucepan should be about halfway up the side of the basin. Once the water is boiling and the steam circulating, reduce the heat slightly so that the water remains at a constant boil but does not bubble up and get into the pudding.

● Top up with more boiling water as it evaporates.

Real egg custard

Custard, or crème anglaise (English cream), is the most delicious accompaniment for sweet pies, tarts and puddings. Made with egg yolks and vanilla, it tastes just wonderful. Adding a little cornflour helps to stabilise the mixture and prevent it from curdling.

Serves 4

300 ml (10 fl oz) semi-skimmed milk
1 vanilla pod, split lengthways
3 egg yolks
1 tbsp caster sugar
1 tsp cornflour

Preparation and cooking time: about 25 minutes

1 Put the milk and vanilla pod into a heavy-based saucepan and heat until just starting to simmer. Remove the pan from the heat and leave to infuse for 10 minutes.

2 Meanwhile, mix together the egg yolks, sugar and cornflour to a smooth paste in a mixing bowl or jug.

3 Remove the vanilla pod from the milk. If liked, scrape the seeds into the milk for a stronger vanilla flavour. Pour the warm milk onto the egg mixture, stirring.

4 Pour back into the pan and cook gently over a low heat, stirring constantly with a wooden spoon, until thick enough to coat the back of the spoon in a thin layer. Do not allow the custard to boil, and remove from the heat as soon as it has thickened. Serve the custard hot or cool.

Some more ideas

● If you don't have a vanilla pod, you can use vanilla caster sugar or add 1 tsp pure vanilla extract to the cooked custard.

● Instead of flavouring the custard with vanilla, infuse the milk with a strip of lemon, orange or lime zest. Or, add 2 tsp instant coffee powder or 30 g (1 oz) grated dark chocolate to the warm milk. Another idea is to stir 1 tbsp liqueur into the cooked custard.

● To make crème pâtissière, increase the sugar to 25 g (scant 1 oz) and the cornflour to 1½ tbsp. This makes a thick custard that can be used as a filling for sweet tarts. Use when cold.

wonderful pies, tarts and puddings

Little Pies and Tarts

Savoury bites for snacks, starters and lunches

Filo is ideal for little pies and tarts as it is so adaptable –
layered into cases for Oriental stir-fried prawns or
wrapped into dainty parcels round a tuna filling. Other
pastries work beautifully too. Choux puffs up into
spectacular buns that are perfect cases for a creamy
guacamole, shortcrust makes pretty tartlets, and easy
scone dough can be fashioned into stylish French
'galettes'. Pies and tarts need not always be made with
pastry, though. Among the tempting variety of little bites
here, you'll find bread dough used
for spicy Mexican-style turkey
pasties, as well as crisp-baked
bread cases filled with a piquant
mackerel and red pepper mixture.

Tomato and basil galettes

Galette is the French term for a flat, round pastry or cake. The galettes here are made from wholemeal scone dough flavoured with a little Parmesan cheese. They make a delicious base for a tomato, basil and pine nut topping. Serve as a snack or starter, or as a light lunch with a mixed leaf salad. They're also good cold.

Serves 6

Parmesan scone dough

115 g (4 oz) self-raising white flour

85 g (3 oz) self-raising wholemeal flour

1 tsp baking powder

pinch of salt

30 g (1 oz) cool butter, diced

25 g (scant 1 oz) Parmesan cheese, freshly grated

120 ml (4 fl oz) semi-skimmed milk

Tomato and basil topping

3 tsp extra virgin olive oil

1 garlic clove, crushed

3 tbsp sun-dried tomato paste

3 tbsp shredded fresh basil leaves

3 large plum tomatoes, thinly sliced

30 g (1 oz) pine nuts

fresh basil leaves to garnish

Preparation time: 20 minutes

Cooking time: 10–12 minutes

1 Preheat the oven to 220ºC (425ºF, gas mark 7). Sift the white and wholemeal flours, baking powder and salt into a bowl, tipping in the bran left in the sieve. Rub in the butter until the mixture resembles fine breadcrumbs. Stir in the Parmesan cheese.

2 Make a well in the middle and pour in the milk. Mix together to make a fairly soft dough. Knead lightly for a few seconds or until smooth.

3 Roll out the dough on a lightly floured surface to 5 mm (¼ in) thickness. Cut out 6 rounds about 10 cm (4 in) in diameter. You will need to re-roll the trimmings to cut out the last round. Transfer the rounds to a non-stick baking sheet, spacing well apart. Mark the edges with a fork, if liked.

4 Brush the tops with 2 tsp of the olive oil. Mix the remaining 1 tsp oil with the garlic, tomato paste and basil, and spread thinly over the rounds, leaving a border of about 5 mm (¼ in) clear. Arrange the tomato slices on top, overlapping them slightly and covering all of the basil topping.

5 Bake for 7 minutes, then scatter the pine nuts over the tomatoes. Return to the oven and bake for 3–5 minutes or until the galettes are risen and the edges are golden brown. Serve hot, garnished with basil leaves.

Another idea

• For caramelised onion galettes, cook 500 g (1 lb 2 oz) thinly sliced red onions in 1½ tbsp extra virgin olive oil over a low heat, partly covered and stirring occasionally, for about 10 minutes. Add 2 tsp balsamic vinegar and 1 tsp soft light brown sugar. Gently cook for a further 4–5 minutes, stirring frequently, until very soft. Remove from the heat and stir in 30 g (1 oz) chopped dry-packed sun-dried tomatoes. Season with pepper to taste. Make the galette bases, adding 2 tsp chopped fresh thyme to the dry ingredients, and rubbing in only 15 g (d oz) butter and 55 g (2 oz) crumbled feta cheese; omit the Parmesan cheese. Spoon the onion mixture on top of the galettes and bake in a preheated 220ºC (425ºF, gas mark 7) oven for 10–12 minutes or until risen and golden brown.

Each serving provides Ⓥ

kcal 240, **protein** 7 g, **fat** 12 g (of which saturated fat 4 g), **carbohydrate** 28 g (of which sugars 4.5 g), **fibre** 3 g

✓✓	copper
✓	A, B₁, E, niacin, calcium, iron, potassium, selenium, zinc

Plus points

• Wholemeal flour contains more B vitamins, iron, selenium and zinc than white flour, but used on its own makes heavy pastry and scone mixtures. Mixing wholemeal and white flour produces a lighter result.

• Apart from its culinary uses, basil is prescribed by herbalists as a natural tranquilliser and to help relieve cramps, upset stomachs and flatulence.

little pies and tarts

Oriental prawn tartlets

These pretty little tartlets, filled with stir-fried prawns and a mixture of crisp, colourful vegetables, make a really unusual light snack or a starter for an Asian meal. The filo tartlet cases can be made ahead, but they are best filled just before serving, so the pastry remains crisp.

Serves 4 (makes 12 tartlets)

1 tbsp sunflower oil

1 tsp toasted sesame oil

3 sheets filo pastry, 30 x 50 cm (12 x 20 in) each, about 90 g (3¼ oz) in total

1 garlic clove, crushed

3 spring onions, thinly sliced

1 tbsp finely chopped fresh root ginger

1 carrot, cut into fine julienne strips

300 g (10½ oz) peeled raw tiger prawns

75 g (2½ oz) mange-tout, sliced diagonally

1 small head pak choy, about 85 g (3 oz), sliced

75 g (2½ oz) bean sprouts

1 tbsp light soy sauce

sprigs of fresh coriander to garnish

Preparation and cooking time: 35–45 minutes

Each serving provides

kcal 183, **protein** 18 g, **fat** 5 g (of which saturated fat 1 g), **carbohydrate** 18 g (of which sugars 3 g), **fibre** 2 g

✓✓✓	B₁₂
✓✓	A, E
✓	C, niacin, calcium, copper, iron, potassium, selenium, zinc

1 Preheat the oven to 200°C (400°F, gas mark 6). Mix together the sunflower and sesame oils. Lay the filo pastry sheets out, one on top of the other. Trim the stacked pastry to make a 30 x 40 cm (12 x 16 in) rectangle (discard the excess pastry). Cut it lengthways into 3 and then across into 4, making 10 cm (4 in) squares. You will have 36 squares of filo.

2 Place 1 filo square in each of the 12 hollows in a non-stick bun tin. Brush very lightly with a little of the oil mixture. Place another square of filo on top, arranging it so the corners are not directly on top of those beneath. Brush with a little more oil, then place a third filo square on top, again with the corners offset. Bake the pastry cases for 5–7 minutes or until they are golden brown and crisp.

3 Meanwhile, heat the remaining oil mixture in a wok or large frying pan. Add the garlic, spring onions and ginger, and stir-fry over a moderate heat for about 30 seconds. Add the carrot and stir-fry for 2 minutes, then add the prawns and stir-fry for 2 more minutes or until they turn pink.

4 Add the mange-tout, pak choy and bean sprouts. Stir-fry over a high heat for 2–3 minutes or until all the vegetables are just tender and the mixture is piping hot. Sprinkle with the soy sauce and toss to mix.

5 Spoon the prawn and vegetable mixture into the filo pastry cases and serve immediately, garnished with sprigs of coriander.

Plus points

• Filo pastry has a lower fat content than other pastries. For example, there are 2 g fat and 275 kcal in 100 g (3½ oz) filo pastry compared to 29 g fat and 449 kcal in the same weight of shortcrust pastry.

• Prawns are a good source of low-fat protein and the antioxidant mineral selenium as well as an excellent source of vitamin B₁₂.

• Mange-tout contain more vitamin C than ordinary garden peas. This is because the pods, which as the name implies are eaten too ('mange-tout' means 'eat all'), make an additional contribution.

little pies and tarts

Some more ideas

• Use peeled prawns instead of tiger prawns. If the prawns are already cooked, add them after stir-frying the vegetables in step 4, and just heat through for 1 minute or so.

• For a vegetarian version, replace the prawns with 300 g (10½ oz) chilled, drained tofu, cut into small cubes. Add at the end of step 3 and stir-fry for 2–3 minutes.

• Replace the pak choy with other leafy greens such as baby spinach leaves or shredded Chinese leaves.

• Try Oriental crab, corn and asparagus tartlets. Instead of sesame oil, mix the sunflower oil with ½ tsp chilli paste. When making the pastry cases, sprinkle lightly between the layered filo squares with 25 g (scant 1 oz) finely chopped peanuts. To make the filling, stir-fry 1 crushed garlic clove, 2 finely chopped shallots and a seeded and finely chopped small hot red chilli in the remaining oil mixture. Stir in 170 g (6 oz) chopped fine asparagus and 100 g (3½ oz) sliced baby corn, and stir-fry for 3–4 minutes or until softened. Add 150 g (5½ oz) fresh or drained, canned white crabmeat and the juice of 1 lime, and stir-fry until hot. Finish by stirring in 2 tbsp chopped fresh coriander.

Puttanesca pizzinis

Home-made mini pizzas topped with a rich tomato, chilli, olive, caper and artichoke mixture will spoil you for anything less. Some crumbled Gorgonzola cheese melted over the top makes a change from the usual mozzarella, and gives these pizzinis a fabulous flavour. Serve with a mixed leaf salad for a delightful lunch or snack.

Serves 6

Oregano pizza dough

450 g (1 lb) strong white (bread) flour

1 tsp dried oregano

1 sachet easy-blend dried yeast, about 7 g

250 ml (8½ fl oz) tepid water, or as needed

Puttanesca topping

1 tbsp extra virgin olive oil

1 red onion, finely chopped

4 garlic cloves, crushed

500 g (1 lb 2 oz) ripe tomatoes, diced

1 fresh red chilli, seeded and finely chopped

50 g (1¾ oz) stoned black and green olives,
　roughly chopped

1 tbsp capers

1 can artichoke hearts, about 400 g, drained
　and quartered

100 g (3½ oz) Gorgonzola cheese,
　crumbled

salt and pepper

Preparation time: 1¾ hours (including rising)
Cooking time: 15 minutes

Each serving provides

kcal 388, **protein** 14 g, **fat** 9.5 g (of which saturated fat 4 g), **carbohydrate** 66 g (of which sugars 6 g), **fibre** 5 g

✓✓✓	selenium
✓✓	B₁, calcium, copper
✓	A, B₆, C, E, folate, niacin, iron, potassium, zinc

1 First make the pizza dough. Sift the flour and ½ tsp salt into a large mixing bowl, and stir in the oregano and yeast. Make a well in the centre and pour in the water. Gradually work the flour mixture into the water to make a soft dough. If it feels too dry, work in a little more water; if the dough sticks to your hand, add a little more flour.

2 Turn out the dough onto a lightly floured work surface and knead for about 10 minutes or until smooth and elastic. Return the dough to the bowl, cover it with a damp tea towel or cling film, and leave to rise in a warm place for 1 hour or until doubled in size.

3 Meanwhile, make the topping. Heat the oil in a medium-sized, heavy-based saucepan and add the onion and garlic. Cook over a low heat for about 10 minutes or until softened, stirring occasionally. Add the tomatoes and chilli, and stir to mix. Cook over a moderate heat for about 25 minutes, stirring occasionally, until very thick.

4 Remove the pan from the heat. Add the olives and capers, and season with salt and pepper to taste. Leave to cool while shaping the pizza bases.

5 Turn out the risen dough onto the lightly floured surface and knock it back. Knead it very lightly, then divide into 6 equal portions. Shape each into a ball, then pat or roll out to a neat disc measuring about 12.5 cm (5 in) across. Arrange the discs, spaced slightly apart, on 2 lightly greased baking trays.

6 Spread the tomato topping evenly over the discs of dough, leaving a 5 mm (¼ in) border clear. Top with the quartered artichokes, then scatter over the Gorgonzola. Leave to rise in a warm place for 15 minutes.

7 Preheat the oven to 230°C (450°F, gas mark 8). Bake the pizzinis for 15 minutes or until the edges of the crust are golden brown and the cheese has melted. Serve hot.

Plus points

• The fat content of olives is relatively high compared to other fruit and vegetables. However, the fat is predominantly unsaturated which is believed to be healthier than the saturated form.

• Artichoke hearts contain a particular type of dietary fibre, called fructoligosaccharides, which encourages the growth of friendly bacteria in the gut.

Some more ideas

• To serve as a starter, divide the dough into 8 equal pieces and shape each into a 10 cm (4 in) diameter disc.

• These pizzinis are equally delicious served cold, to take on a picnic or to include in a packed lunch.

• Replace 50 g (1¾ oz) of the white flour with rye flour or Granary (malted brown bread) flour.

• To make an aubergine pizza tart, press out the risen dough in a Swiss roll tin that measures 22 x 30 cm (8½ x 12 in). Spread over the chilli tomato sauce. Instead of the artichokes, use 1 large aubergine, cut into 1 cm (½ in) dice and tossed with 1 tbsp extra virgin olive oil, 1 tbsp chopped fresh thyme or marjoram and seasoning to taste. Scatter over the tomato sauce and top with 100 g (3½ oz) diced mozzarella. Leave to rise for 15 minutes, then bake for 20–25 minutes or until the edges of the crust are golden brown and the topping is bubbling and golden. Cool for 2 minutes, then cut into 6 squares or 12 slices and serve, garnished with fresh basil leaves.

Smoked mackerel, roasted pepper and horseradish croustades

Slices of bread, lightly brushed with butter and then baked in bun tins, make perfect little 'cups' for a piquant red pepper and mackerel filling. Served with rocket tossed in a lemon vinaigrette, they make a very appealing starter. The bread cases and filling can be made ahead, then assembled just before serving.

Serves 6 (makes 12 croustades)

1 red pepper, halved and seeded
6 large slices of oatmeal bread
15 g (½ oz) butter, melted
150 g (5½ oz) reduced-fat soft cheese
1 tbsp hot horseradish sauce
75 g (2½ oz) skinless smoked mackerel fillet,
    flaked into large pieces
salt and pepper
fresh dill sprigs or snipped chives to garnish
Rocket salad
2 tbsp extra virgin olive oil
juice of ½ lemon
½ tsp Dijon mustard
pinch of caster sugar
125 g (4½ oz) rocket leaves

Preparation and cooking time: 40–45 minutes

Each serving provides
kcal 219, **protein** 8 g, **fat** 14 g (of which saturated fat 5 g), **carbohydrate** 16 g (of which sugars 4 g), **fibre** 2 g

✓✓✓	C
✓✓	A, B$_{12}$
✓	B$_6$, folate, niacin

1 Preheat the oven to 190°C (375°F, gas mark 5). Place the pepper cut side down on a baking sheet and roast in the oven for 15 minutes. Put the pepper into a polythene bag and set aside for 15 minutes or until it is cool enough to handle.

2 Meanwhile, trim the crusts thinly from the bread and discard, then roll over the bread slices with a rolling pin to flatten them. Using a fluted 7.5 cm (3 in) round biscuit cutter, cut out 2 rounds from each slice.

3 Lightly grease the 12 hollows of a deep bun tin using a little of the melted butter. Brush the remaining butter over one side of each bread round and press it into a hollow in the tin, buttered side up. Bake the bread cases for about 12 minutes or until crisp and golden. Leave to cool.

4 Peel the pepper and finely chop the flesh. Mix with the soft cheese and horseradish sauce. Season with salt and pepper to taste. Set aside.

5 For the salad, whisk together the olive oil, lemon juice, mustard, sugar, and seasoning to taste in a mixing bowl. Add the rocket and toss, then arrange on serving plates.

6 Spoon the cheese mixture into the bread cases and top each one with flakes of mackerel. Set 2 croustades on each plate. Garnish with dill or chives and serve immediately.

Another idea

• Make smoked salmon and goat's cheese croustades, using soft-grain bread for the cases. For the filling, coarsely grate 100 g (3½ oz) cucumber and squeeze thoroughly in your hands to remove excess juice. Beat the cucumber into 170 g (6 oz) soft goat's cheese together with 2 tsp chopped capers, 1 tbsp snipped fresh chives, and salt and pepper to taste. Pile the filling into the bread cases, top with 75 g (2½ oz) smoked salmon strips and garnish with chives.

Plus points

• Mackerel is very nutritious, providing vitamins B$_2$, B$_6$, D and niacin as well as iodine and potassium. These nutrients are not destroyed by the smoking process.
• Horseradish is used in herbal medicine as an aid to digestion.

Souffléd salmon and dill tartlets

Individual tartlets served with a salad garnish make a very appealing starter. This fish filling is wonderfully light as it's made with a cornflour-thickened sauce, without the addition of fat, and whisked egg whites are folded in for an airy soufflé-like texture. Serve straight from the oven to really impress.

Serves 6

Shortcrust pastry

115 g (4 oz) plain flour

55 g (2 oz) cool butter, diced

Salmon filling

25 g (scant 1 oz) cornflour

150 ml (5 fl oz) semi-skimmed milk

1 can skinless, boneless pink salmon, about 180 g, drained and flaked

2 tbsp chopped fresh dill

2 tbsp snipped fresh chives

2 eggs, separated

salt and pepper

To serve

150 g (5½ oz) mixed salad leaves, such as frisée and rocket

1 red pepper, seeded and cut into thin strips

Preparation time: 40 minutes, plus at least 30 minutes chilling

Cooking time: 15 minutes

Each serving provides

kcal 236, **protein** 11 g, **fat** 12 g (of which saturated fat 6 g), **carbohydrate** 22 g (of which sugars 4 g), **fibre** 1 g

✓✓✓ A, B₁₂, C

✓ E, niacin, calcium, selenium, zinc

1 To make the pastry, sift the flour and a pinch of salt into a large bowl. Rub in the butter until the mixture resembles breadcrumbs. Sprinkle with 2 tbsp cold water and mix with a round-bladed knife to form a dough. Gather the dough into a smooth ball, then wrap in greaseproof paper or cling film and chill for at least 30 minutes. Meanwhile, start preparing the filling.

2 Blend the cornflour with 2 tbsp of the milk to make a smooth paste. Heat the remaining milk in a saucepan to boiling point. Pour a little of the hot milk into the cornflour mixture, stirring. Return this to the milk in the saucepan. Bring to the boil, stirring until the sauce thickens, then reduce the heat and simmer gently for 2 minutes.

3 Remove the pan from the heat. Stir in the salmon, dill, chives, and salt and pepper to taste. Mix in the egg yolks. Set aside.

4 Preheat the oven to 200°C (400°F, gas mark 6). Cut the pastry dough into 6 pieces. Roll out each thinly and use to line 6 individual, loose-bottomed, non-stick tartlet tins 9 cm (3½ in) in diameter and 2.5 cm (1 in) deep.

5 Prick the tartlet cases, then place on a baking sheet. Bake 'blind' (see page 19) for 10 minutes. Remove the paper and beans, and bake for a further 5 minutes or until lightly golden. Allow to cool, then carefully remove the tartlet cases from the tins and set them back on the baking sheet.

6 Whisk the egg whites until stiff, then fold into the salmon mixture. Pile the mixture into the tartlet cases and bake for 15 minutes or until well risen and golden. Serve immediately on individual plates, garnished with the salad leaves and strips of pepper.

Plus points

• Like other oily fish, salmon is a good source of omega-3 fatty acids, which can help to protect against heart disease and strokes.

• The thick sauce (panada) used as the base for the soufflé filling is thickened with cornflour rather than the classic butter and flour roux, and so is much lower in fat.

• Dill has been used for its soothing and sedative properties since Egyptian times. It became known in America as 'meeting house seeds', as dill seeds were chewed by early settlers to prevent tummy rumbles when sermons went on too long.

little pies and tarts

Some more ideas

• Instead of salmon, use canned tuna in spring water, well drained.

• Serve the tartlets cold. They will not have a soufflé appearance, but will still be delicious.

• For souffléd spinach and Pamesan tartlets, cook 125 g (4½ oz) frozen spinach over a low heat for 2 minutes or until thawed. Squeeze out excess moisture, then add to the sauce together with ½ tsp grated nutmeg; omit the salmon, dill and chives. Mix in the egg yolks and 30 g (1 oz) freshly grated Parmesan cheese. Fold in the egg whites, then bake as in the main recipe. Serve garnished with salad leaves, cherry tomatoes and spring onions.

Spicy filo triangles

Here's a quick version of the popular Indian samosas, baked rather than deep-fried for a healthy, light result. The crisp filo pastry parcels contain a curry-spiced vegetable filling, and they are served hot from the oven with a fresh mango and ginger salsa to make a scrumptious starter or light snack.

Serves 4 (makes 12 triangles)

2 sheets filo pastry, 30 x 50 cm (12 x 20 in) each, about 60 g (2¼ oz) in total

1 tbsp sunflower oil

½ tsp coriander seeds, coarsely crushed

Vegetable filling

1 potato, about 170 g (6 oz), peeled and diced

1 small carrot, peeled and diced

55 g (2 oz) frozen peas

1 tbsp curry paste

1 tbsp chopped fresh coriander

pinch of salt

Mango and ginger salsa

1 ripe but firm mango

½ tsp grated fresh root ginger

1 tsp lemon juice

1 tsp caster sugar

¼ tsp crushed dried chillies

1 tsp sunflower oil

Preparation time: 35 minutes

Cooking time: about 15 minutes

Each serving provides   Ⓥ

kcal 156, **protein** 4 g, **fat** 5 g (of which saturated fat 0.5 g), **carbohydrate** 25.5 g (of which sugars 8 g), **fibre** 3 g

✓✓✓	A
✓✓	C
✓	B₁, B₆, E

1 To make the filling, cook the diced potato and carrot in a saucepan of boiling water for 5 minutes. Add the peas and cook for a further 2 minutes. Drain well and tip the vegetables into a bowl. Stir in the curry paste, coriander and salt, mashing the mixture very slightly to combine. Leave to cool.

2 Preheat the oven to 200°C (400°F, gas mark 6). Taking one sheet of filo pastry at a time (keeping the other sheet covered to prevent it from drying out), cut it widthways into 6 strips, each 30 cm (12 in) long. Brush them with a little of the oil.

3 Lay one of the pastry strips lengthways in front of you and put a rounded tbsp of the filling in the middle of the end nearest to you. Pick up one end corner and fold it diagonally over the filling to make a triangular shape, flattening the filling slightly. Continue folding the strip over in a triangular shape until you come almost to the end. Trim off excess pastry from the end. Repeat with the remaining filo pastry and filling to make 12 triangles in all.

4 Place the filo triangles on a non-stick baking sheet, brush the tops with the remaining oil and scatter over the crushed coriander seeds. Bake for 10–15 minutes or until golden.

5 Meanwhile, make the salsa. Cut the mango flesh from both sides of the flat central stone, then peel the flesh and cut into small dice. Mix in a bowl with the ginger, lemon juice, sugar, chillies and oil. Serve the salsa with the hot filo triangles.

Plus points

• Using vegetables in novel and tasty ways, such as in this filling for crisp savoury pastries, can help to boost intake so that the recommended 5 portions of fruit and vegetables a day can easily be achieved.

• Fresh mangoes are an excellent source of beta-carotene, which the body can convert into vitamin A. Beta-carotene also acts as a powerful antioxidant, helping to protect the body from heart disease and cancer.

• Frozen peas are likely to be more nutritious than fresh peas, as they are frozen straight after picking and podding. In particular, their vitamin C content is higher.

Some more ideas

- Serve the triangles as party food. They can be made ahead and then reheated in a 190°C (375°F, gas mark 5) oven for 10 minutes.
- For Thai-style chicken curry spring rolls, cook the potato and peas (omit the carrot), then mix with 115 g (4 oz) cooked skinless, boneless chicken, finely chopped, 2 chopped spring onions, 1 tbsp Thai green curry paste and a pinch of salt. Cut the filo pastry sheets in half lengthways, then into 4 crossways to make sixteen 12.5 x 15 cm (5 x 6 in) pieces. Brush lightly with sunflower oil. For each roll, spread a tbsp of the filling along a short side of a piece of filo to make a plump sausage shape. Fold over the long sides by 1 cm (½ in), then roll up like a cigar. Set the rolls join side down on a baking sheet. Brush with oil, sprinkle with the coriander seeds and bake as in the main recipe. Serve 4 rolls each with a plum dipping sauce: dissolve 30 g (1 oz) sugar in 3 tbsp water, then add 3 large, ripe, red-skinned plums, chopped. Bring to the boil and bubble for 5 minutes or until very soft, stirring often. Press the mixture through a sieve. Stir in 1 tbsp cider or white wine vinegar, then return to the pan and boil for 2 minutes. Cool before serving.

Guacamole choux buns

Savoury choux buns look spectacular, yet are easy to make. Here they are filled with a creamy mixture of avocado, tomato, cucumber and cannellini beans flavoured with lime juice, fresh coriander and a touch of garlic. They make an appealing and well-balanced lunch dish, delightful with a glass of fruity white wine.

Serves 5

1 quantity Choux pastry (see page 23)

2 Little Gem lettuces, separated into leaves

Guacamole and bean filling

1 can cannellini beans, about 410 g, drained
    and rinsed

2 small avocados

juice of 1 lime

1 large tomato, seeded and finely diced

½ red onion, finely chopped

12.5 cm (5 in) piece of cucumber, finely diced

1 garlic clove, crushed

2 tbsp chopped fresh coriander

salt

cayenne pepper

Preparation time: 40 minutes (including making
    the pastry)

Cooking time: about 25 minutes

Each serving provides ⓥ

kcal 313, **protein** 10 g, **fat** 20 g (of which
saturated fat 8.5 g), **carbohydrate** 24 g (of
which sugars 5 g), **fibre** 6 g

✓✓	A, E
✓	B₁, B₂, B₆, B₁₂, C, folate, calcium, copper, iron, potassium, selenium, zinc

1 Preheat the oven to 220°C (425°F, gas mark 7). Spoon the choux pastry in 5 equal mounds on a large greased baking tray, spacing the mounds well apart. Use the spoon to make the mounds about 7.5 cm (3 in) across and 3 cm (1¼ in) high. Bake them for 18–20 minutes or until well risen and golden brown.

2 Remove the baking tray from the oven. Make a small hole in the side of each bun, using a skewer or the point of a small knife, then return to the oven. Bake for a further 5 minutes. Transfer the buns to a wire rack to cool.

3 Meanwhile, make the filling. Tip the beans into a mixing bowl and mash with a potato masher until quite smooth. Cut the avocados in half, remove the stones and scoop out the flesh into another bowl. Mash the flesh fairly roughly using a fork, then stir into the beans together with the lime juice.

4 Add the tomato, onion, cucumber, garlic and chopped coriander to the bean and avocado mixture. Season with salt and cayenne pepper to taste. Mix together well.

5 Just before serving, split open the choux buns and fill with the guacamole and bean mixture. Place them on individual serving plates garnished with lettuce leaves.

Another idea

• To make crunchy hummus-filled choux buns, purée 1 can of chickpeas, about 410 g, drained and rinsed, in a food processor or blender with 1 tbsp tahini, 1 crushed garlic clove and the juice of 1 lemon. Stir in a 10 cm (4 in) piece of cucumber, finely diced, 1 grated carrot, 2 finely chopped spring onions and 1 seeded and finely diced red pepper. Season with ½ tsp ground cumin, and salt and pepper to taste. Spoon into the choux buns. Garnish with radicchio leaves and serve with a tomato salad.

Plus points

• Cannellini beans, like other pulses, are an excellent source of protein and starchy carbohydrate, while being low in fat.

• Avocados are unusual in that they are fruits that contain a large amount of fat. The fat is predominantly monounsaturated, however, particularly in the form of oleic acid. This can help to lower levels of the harmful LDL cholesterol while raising levels of the beneficial HDL cholesterol.

• Lime juice contains vitamin C, which will help to improve the absorption of iron from the cannellini beans.

Turkey empanadas

There are lots of different variations on these savoury Mexican pastries, which are similar to Cornish pasties.
The filling here is a blend of lean turkey and vegetables, subtly flavoured with spices, nuts and dried fruit.

Serves 5

175 ml (6 fl oz) warm water

1 packet white bread or pizza dough mix,
   about 250 g

1 small egg, beaten

¼ tsp paprika

Spicy turkey filling

1 tbsp sunflower oil

1 onion, thinly sliced

1 garlic clove, crushed

1 fresh green or red chilli, seeded and finely
   chopped

250 g (8½ oz) minced turkey

300 g (10½ oz) potatoes, peeled and cut into
   1 cm (½ in) dice

½ tsp ground cinnamon

½ tsp ground coriander

½ tsp ground cumin

4 tbsp dry sherry or white wine

1 large carrot, coarsely grated

45 g (1½ oz) raisins

30 g (1 oz) blanched almonds, toasted and
   roughly chopped

2 tbsp tomato purée

2 tbsp chopped fresh coriander

salt and pepper

Preparation time: about 30 minutes, plus
   10–15 minutes rising

Cooking time: 25 minutes

1 First make the filling. Heat the oil in a frying pan and cook the onion, garlic and chilli on a fairly high heat for 2–3 minutes, stirring, until softened and lightly browned. Add the turkey mince and stir for a further 4–5 minutes.

2 Meanwhile, part-cook the diced potatoes in a saucepan of boiling water for 5 minutes. Drain well.

3 Stir the cinnamon, coriander and cumin into the turkey mixture and cook for 30 seconds. Add the sherry or wine and simmer for 2–3 minutes or until most of the liquid has evaporated.

4 Stir in the potatoes, carrot, raisins, almonds, tomato purée, chopped coriander, and salt and pepper to taste. Remove from the heat.

5 Stir the water into the bread mix and knead for 2 minutes or until smooth. Cover and leave to rest for 5 minutes, then divide into 5 equal pieces. Roll out each piece on a lightly floured surface to a 20 cm (8 in) round.

6 Preheat the oven to 220°C (425°F, gas mark 7). Divide the filling among the dough rounds, spooning it into the centre. Brush the edge of each round with beaten egg, then fold over into a half-moon shape. Press the edges together and roll over to seal. Place on a non-stick baking sheet, cover with oiled cling film and leave in a warm place for 10–15 minutes or until slightly risen.

7 Uncover the empanadas, glaze them with the rest of the beaten egg and sprinkle with the paprika. Bake for 10 minutes, then reduce the temperature to 180°C (350°F, gas mark 4) and bake for a further 15 minutes. Serve hot or at room temperature.

Plus points

- Turkey mince contains less fat than beef or lamb mince and even less fat than chicken, making it one of the lowest fat meats available.
- White bread and pizza dough are both good sources of starchy carbohydrate. Recommendations are that at least half the calories in a healthy diet should come from starchy foods.
- Raisins, like other dried fruits, are very good sources of dietary fibre. They are also virtually fat-free and provide useful amounts of iron.

Each serving provides

kcal 424, protein 24 g, **fat 10 g** (of which saturated fat 2 g), **carbohydrate 58 g** (of which sugars 12 g), **fibre 5 g**

✓✓✓	A, copper, selenium
✓✓	B₁, B₆, B₁₂, E, niacin, zinc
✓	B₂, C, folate, calcium, iron, potassium

little pies and tarts

46

Some more ideas

• Sprinkle the empanadas with poppy seeds instead of paprika.

• Make a large pie instead of pasties. Roll out about two-thirds of the dough and use to line a greased 23 cm (9 in) shallow pie dish. Add the filling, smoothing the surface evenly. Moisten the edges with beaten egg. Roll out the remaining dough and use to cover the pie, sealing the edges firmly. Make a steam hole in the centre of the dough lid. Allow to rise in a warm place for 10–15 minutes, then glaze with beaten egg. Bake for 10 minutes. Reduce the heat and bake for a further 20–25 minutes. Serve cut in slices.

• For red bean and pepper empanadas, cook 1 thinly sliced onion in 1 tbsp extra virgin olive oil for 2 minutes. Stir in 1 seeded and finely chopped fresh red chilli, 1 seeded and diced red pepper and 1 seeded and diced yellow pepper. Cook on a moderate heat for 4–5 minutes. Add 1 diced courgette and cook for 2–3 minutes to soften. Stir in 2 diced tomatoes, 1 can red kidney beans, about 410 g, drained and rinsed, 1 tsp fennel seeds, 2 tbsp chopped fresh basil, and salt and pepper to taste. Use to fill the empanadas and bake as in the main recipe.

Polenta and mushroom grills

Cooked and cooled polenta can be cut into shapes and grilled to make an excellent base for a tempting topping. Here the polenta is flavoured with Gruyère cheese, and the topping is a savoury mixture of mushrooms, walnuts and herbs. Serve as a sophisticated starter, with a few mixed salad leaves if you like.

Serves 6 (makes 12 polenta grills)

750 ml (1¼ pints) vegetable stock
170 g (6 oz) instant polenta
85 g (3 oz) Gruyère cheese, grated
15 g (½ oz) dried porcini mushrooms
3 tbsp extra virgin olive oil
225 g (8 oz) chestnut mushrooms, sliced
3 tbsp dry sherry
2 tbsp chopped fresh flat-leaf parsley, plus extra to garnish
2 tsp chopped fresh rosemary
30 g (1 oz) walnuts, finely chopped
salt and pepper

Preparation and cooking time: 45 minutes, plus 1 hour cooling

Each serving provides

kcal 203, **protein** 4 g, **fat** 9 g (of which saturated fat 1 g), **carbohydrate** 23.5 g (of which sugars 0.5 g), **fibre** 3 g

✓✓✓	copper
✓	selenium

1 Bring the stock to the boil in a large saucepan. Pour in the polenta in a steady stream, stirring with a wooden spoon to prevent lumps from forming. Cook over a low heat, stirring constantly, for about 5 minutes or until the mixture thickens and pulls away from the sides of the pan. Remove from the heat and stir in the Gruyère cheese. Season with salt and pepper to taste.

2 Pour the polenta onto a damp baking tray and spread out into a rectangle measuring about 20 x 18 cm (8 x 7 in) and about 1 cm (½ in) thick. Leave to cool for 1 hour or until set.

3 Meanwhile, put the dried porcini mushrooms in a bowl and cover with boiling water. Leave to soak for 20 minutes. Drain, reserving 2 tbsp of the soaking liquid. Finely chop the mushrooms.

4 Preheat the grill to moderately hot. Lightly brush the polenta rectangle all over with 1 tbsp of the oil. Cut into 12 fingers, each measuring 5 x 6 cm (2 x 2½ in), trimming the edges to straighten them. Place oiled side up on the rack in the grill pan, and grill for 5 minutes or until lightly browned.

5 Turn the polenta slices over and grill for a further 2–3 minutes or until lightly browned. Remove from the grill and keep hot.

6 Heat the remaining 2 tbsp oil in a frying pan. Add the soaked dried mushrooms and the sliced chestnut mushrooms, and sauté over a fairly high heat for 3–4 minutes or until softened.

7 Add the sherry and the reserved mushroom soaking liquid. Cook over a high heat for 1–2 minutes, stirring, until most of the liquid has evaporated. Add the parsley, rosemary, walnuts, and salt and pepper to taste.

8 Spoon the mushroom mixture on top of the warm polenta fingers. Garnish with a little chopped parsley and serve immediately.

Plus points

• Polenta is fine corn or maize meal. It provides a starchy carbohydrate alternative for those who need to avoid wheat or gluten in their diet.

• All mushrooms are a good source of copper, a mineral with many functions but particularly needed for the maintenance of healthy bones.

• Walnuts are a good source of many of the antioxidant nutrients, including selenium, zinc, copper and vitamin E.

little pies and tarts

48

Some more ideas

• Add 2–3 tbsp crème fraîche to the mushroom mixture with the herbs and walnuts, and heat.

• Replace 150 ml (5 fl oz) of the stock with dry white wine.

• Add 1 tsp chilli powder or cayenne pepper to the cooked polenta at the end of step 2.

• Cut the cooled and set polenta into smaller shapes and serve as tasty party nibbles.

• Make polenta and tapenade squares. Cut the cooled and set polenta into squares (or other shapes) and grill as in the main recipe. For the tapenade topping, blend together 85 g (3 oz) stoned black olives, 2 tbsp capers, 30 g (1 oz) sun-dried tomatoes packed in oil, well drained, 1 crushed garlic clove, 3 tbsp extra virgin olive oil, 2 tbsp chopped fresh flat-leaf parsley, and salt and pepper to taste in a food processor. Alternatively, finely chop the olives, capers and tomatoes, and mix with the garlic, oil, parsley and seasoning.

Tunisian tuna and egg briks

These dainty pastry parcels are traditionally made with a special pastry called malsouka and deep-fried, but baked filo pastry gives very good results and is much lower in fat. With a tomato and cucumber salad, and some fruit chutney alongside, they make a really delicious lunch.

Serves 4 (makes 8 briks)

2½ tbsp extra virgin olive oil

8 spring onions, thinly sliced

200 g (7 oz) baby spinach leaves, roughly torn

4 sheets filo pastry, 30 x 50 cm (12 x 20 in) each, about 120 g (4¼ oz) in total

1 can tuna in spring water, about 200 g, drained and flaked

2 eggs, hard-boiled and finely chopped

dash of hot pepper sauce

salt and pepper

To serve

4 ripe tomatoes, chopped

½ cucumber, chopped

1 tbsp lemon juice

4 tbsp mango or apricot chutney

Preparation time: 30 minutes

Cooking time: 12–15 minutes

Each serving provides

kcal 339, **protein** 21 g, **fat** 12 g (of which saturated fat 2 g), **carbohydrate** 39 g (of which sugars 20 g), **fibre** 3 g

✓✓✓	A, B$_{12}$, selenium
✓✓	C, E, folate, niacin
✓	B$_1$, B$_2$, B$_6$, calcium, iron, potassium, zinc

1 Heat 2 tsp of the oil in a large saucepan and cook the spring onions over a low heat for 3 minutes or until beginning to soften. Add the spinach, cover with a tight-fitting lid and cook for a further 2–3 minutes or until tender and wilted, stirring once or twice. Tip the mixture into a sieve or colander and leave to drain and cool.

2 Using a saucer as a guide, cut out 24 rounds about 12.5 cm (5 in) in diameter from the filo pastry, cutting 6 rounds from each sheet. Stack the filo rounds in a pile, then cover with cling film to prevent them from drying out.

3 When the spinach mixture is cool, squeeze out as much excess liquid as possible, then transfer to a bowl. Add the tuna, eggs, hot pepper sauce, and salt and pepper to taste. Mix well.

4 Preheat the oven to 200°C (400°F, gas mark 6). Take one filo round and very lightly brush with some of the remaining oil. Top with a second round and brush with a little oil, then place a third round on top and brush with oil.

5 Place a heaped tbsp of the filling in the middle of the round, then fold the pastry over to make a half-moon shape. Fold in the edges, twisting them to seal, and place on a non-stick baking sheet. Repeat with the remaining pastry and filling to make 8 briks in all.

6 Lightly brush the briks with the remaining oil. Bake for 12–15 minutes or until the pastry is crisp and golden brown.

7 Meanwhile, combine the tomatoes and cucumber in a bowl and sprinkle with the lemon juice and seasoning to taste. Serve the briks hot with this salad and the chutney.

Some more ideas

• Serve with plain low-fat yogurt rather than fruit chutney.

• For Turkish boreks with feta and tomato, cut the filo pastry into twenty-four 12.5 cm (5 in) squares. For the filling, crumble 200 g (7 oz) feta cheese and mix with 3 seeded and chopped plum tomatoes, 30 g (1 oz) toasted flaked almonds, 2 tbsp chopped fresh coriander, 2 tsp chopped fresh mint and seasoning to taste. For each borek, layer 3 pastry squares, brushing each with a little oil, add a spoonful of filling, and bring the 4 corners together over the top, pinching to seal. Brush with the remaining oil and bake as in the main recipe.

Plus point

• Using tuna canned in spring water, rather than in oil, helps to keep the fat content of the dish healthily low.

little pies and tarts

50

Goat's cheese, cranberry and oatmeal tartlets

Adding rolled oats to shortcrust pastry not only makes it more nutritious, it also gives it more texture. The little pastry cases have a delectable tart-sweet filling of cranberry sauce, goat's cheese and a yogurt custard. They make a fine lunch dish. Serve with a crisp mixed leaf salad.

Serves 6

1 quantity Oatmeal shortcrust pastry (see Some more ideas, page 22), chilled for at least 30 minutes

Filling

3 large eggs

120 ml (4 fl oz) plain low-fat yogurt

300 ml (10 fl oz) semi-skimmed milk

4 tbsp cranberry sauce

3 tbsp snipped fresh chives

85 g (3 oz) goat's cheese, crumbled

salt and pepper

Preparation time: 45 minutes (including making the pastry), plus at least 30 minutes chilling

Cooking time: 25–30 minutes

Each serving provides Ⓥ

kcal 363, **protein** 13 g, **fat** 20 g (of which saturated fat 11 g), **carbohydrate** 36 g (of which sugars 15 g), **fibre** 1 g

✓✓ A, B$_{12}$, calcium

✓ B$_1$, B$_2$, E, folate, niacin, copper, zinc

1 Preheat the oven to 190°C (375°F, gas mark 5). Cut the pastry dough into 6 pieces. Roll out each piece thinly on a lightly floured surface and use to line 6 individual, loose-bottomed, non-stick tartlet tins 12.5 cm (5 in) in diameter and 2.5 cm (1 in) deep.

2 Prick the tartlet cases and place on a baking sheet, then 'bake blind' (see page 19) for 12 minutes. Remove the paper and beans, and return to the oven to bake for a further 8–10 minutes or until light golden brown. Remove from the oven. Lower the temperature to 180°C (350°F, gas mark 4).

3 Lightly beat the eggs in a small mixing bowl. Add the yogurt, milk, and salt and pepper to taste, and mix well together.

4 Spread 2 tsp of the cranberry sauce in the bottom of each pastry case, then scatter over the chives and goat's cheese. Pour the egg mixture into the pastry cases, dividing it equally among them. Bake for 25–30 minutes or until the filling is slightly puffed up and golden brown. Serve warm.

Another idea

• For ricotta and watercress tartlets, spread 1½ tsp red pesto sauce in the bottom of each baked pastry case. Divide 100 g (3½ oz) chopped watercress and 6 tbsp chopped sun-dried tomatoes packed in oil, well drained, among the cases. For the custard, beat the eggs with the milk and 115 g (4 oz) ricotta cheese. Pour into the pastry cases, then bake as in the main recipe.

Plus points

• Whether a cheese is made from goat's milk, cow's milk or another milk, it provides protein, calcium and phosphorus as well as several B vitamins.

• Cranberries are not only a rich source of vitamin C, they also contain a natural antibiotic which helps to control some urinary tract infections, mostly notably cystitis.

• Rolled oats are made from the whole oat grain with only the husk removed before they are rolled flat. The nutritional value of the whole grain is therefore retained.

Ham and wild rice pastries

The flavours of smoky, dry-cured Black Forest ham, shiitake and chestnut mushrooms, and courgettes work well with wild rice in the filling for these delicious filo pastries. If you're looking for an interesting lunch dish, this recipe certainly fits the bill and just needs a side salad to serve with it.

Serves 4

5 sheets filo pastry, 30 x 50 cm (12 x 20 in) each, about 150 g (5½ oz) in total
30 g (1 oz) butter, melted
2 tsp poppy seeds

Filling

100 g (3½ oz) mixed basmati and wild rice
300 ml (10 fl oz) chicken stock
1 tbsp extra virgin olive oil
1 red onion, finely chopped
100 g (3½ oz) shiitake mushrooms, sliced
100 g (3½ oz) chestnut mushrooms, sliced
2 small courgettes, diced
140 g (5 oz) Black Forest ham, trimmed of fat and snipped into strips
2 tsp chopped fresh tarragon (optional)
salt and pepper

Preparation time: 40 minutes
Cooking time: 10 minutes

Each serving provides

kcal 352, **protein** 16 g, **fat** 13 g (of which saturated fat 5 g), **carbohydrate** 47 g (of which sugars 2 g), **fibre** 1 g

✓✓	copper
✓	A, B$_1$, B$_2$, B$_6$, C, folate, niacin, potassium, selenium, zinc

1 Preheat the oven to 190°C (375°F, gas mark 5). For the filling, put the rice into a saucepan, pour over the stock and bring to the boil. Reduce the heat to low, then cover and simmer gently for 20 minutes, or according to the packet instructions, until the rice is tender.

2 Meanwhile, heat the oil in a large non-stick frying pan. Add the onion, mushrooms and courgettes, cover and cook for 6–8 minutes, stirring occasionally, until softened. Leave to cool while you prepare the pastry.

3 Lay 4 of the filo pastry sheets out, one on top of the other. (Keep the fifth sheet covered so it doesn't dry out). Trim the stacked filo to make a 30 x 45 cm (12 x 18 in) rectangle. Cut it lengthways in half and then across into 3 to make 15 cm (6 in) squares. You will have 24 squares.

4 Place 4 of the squares on the work surface and brush very lightly with butter. Place another 4 squares on top at a slight angle and butter them. Repeat the layering to make 4 rough piles, each with 6 buttered squares of pastry.

5 Add the rice and ham to the mushroom mixture. Stir in the tarragon, if using, and season with salt and pepper to taste. Divide the mushroom mixture among the filo stacks, spooning it into the centre. Lift up the pastry edges to contain but not completely enclose the filling – the parcels should still be open at the top. Place on a non-stick baking sheet.

6 Cut the remaining sheet of filo pastry in half lengthways and then across into thin strips. Brush the strips with the remaining butter, then scrunch them up and place on top of the parcels to cover the filling.

7 Scatter over the poppy seeds. Bake for 10 minutes or until the pastry is crisp and golden brown. Serve hot.

Plus points

• Over 2,500 varieties of mushrooms are grown throughout the world, though not all are edible. They provide useful amounts of many of the B vitamins and only contain 0.5 g fat and 13 kcal in 100 g (3½ oz).
• Wild rice is cultivated from the seeds of a North American wild aquatic grass. It contains more protein than 'true' varieties of rice.
• Ham is a good source of protein and vitamin B. The fat content can be reduced by trimming off any visible fat.

Some more ideas

• These pastries can be prepared ahead, up to the end of step 7, and kept chilled. Bake just before serving, adding an extra 3–5 minutes to the cooking time.

• To make spicy chorizo, rice and olive pastries, cook 100 g (3½ oz) white long-grain rice in a covered pan with 6 shredded dry-packed, sun-dried tomatoes and 250 ml (8½ fl oz) chicken stock for 10–15 minutes or until the rice is tender and all the stock has been absorbed. Meanwhile, combine 100 g (3½ oz) chopped chorizo sausage, 1 finely chopped red onion and 1 seeded and diced red pepper in a frying pan, cover and cook for 6–8 minutes or until the onion is tender. Add the rice mixture, 45 g (1½ oz) sliced black olives, 1 can sweetcorn, about 200 g, drained, 20 fresh basil leaves, roughly torn up, and seasoning to taste. Use to fill the filo pastries. Scatter over 2 tsp sesame seeds and bake as in the main recipe.

Simple Family Meals

Main dishes to please all ages

The appetising and satisfying dishes here are sure to become firm favourites. Children will love the pizza dough tart filled with ricotta and cherry tomatoes, and the pie made from layers of tortillas and chicken chilli. For a Sunday lunch that all the family will enjoy, why not try a warming beef and chestnut pie with a suetcrust lid, or a lamb hotpot topped with herbed scone triangles?

Savoury little rice puddings, rich with Cheddar and asparagus, make a great midweek meal. And who could resist a mash-topped pie with a chicken, apple and cider filling?

Potato tart with tuna, chorizo and black olives

This pizza-style tart uses potato pastry as a base, and is topped with an appetising mélange of tuna, spicy chorizo sausage, peppers and olives. Toppings can easily be varied to include your own favourites. Serve with a salad – watercress and cherry tomato is good – for an easy family meal.

Serves 4

1 quantity Herbed potato pastry, flavoured with 1 tbsp chopped fresh basil (see Some more ideas, page 24), chilled for 30 minutes

Tuna and chorizo filling

8 shallots

100 g (3½ oz) chorizo sausage, thinly sliced

1 red pepper, seeded and thinly sliced

1 yellow pepper, seeded and thinly sliced

140 g (5 oz) tomato passata

1 can tuna in spring water, about 200 g, drained and flaked

30 g (1 oz) stoned black olives, halved

Preparation time: about 1 hour (including making the pastry), plus 30 minutes chilling
Cooking time: 15 minutes

Each serving provides

kcal 408, **protein** 20 g, **fat** 19 g (of which saturated fat 10 g), **carbohydrate** 42 g (of which sugars 8.5 g), **fibre** 4 g

✓✓✓	A, B₁₂, C, selenium
✓✓	B₆, folate, niacin
✓	B₁, E, calcium, copper, iron, potassium, zinc

1 Preheat the oven to 190°C (375°F, gas mark 5). For the filling, place the shallots in a heatproof bowl and pour over enough boiling water to cover. Leave for about 5 minutes, then drain. When the shallots are cool enough to handle, peel and quarter.

2 Place the potato pastry dough on a non-stick baking sheet and roll out to a 28 cm (11 in) round. Bake for 20–25 minutes or until light golden.

3 Meanwhile, gently cook the chorizo in a non-stick frying pan. When the oil starts to run from the sausage, add the shallots and cook for 2–3 minutes or until the shallots are glazed. Add the red and yellow peppers, and cook for a further 1–2 minutes to soften.

4 Spread the passata evenly over the surface of the pastry round, leaving a border clear. Top with the shallot, pepper and chorizo mixture. Scatter over the tuna and olives.

5 Bake the tart for 15 minutes or until the exposed edge is golden brown. Serve hot, cut into wedges.

Another idea

• For a potato tart with sardines and red onion, spread the tomato passata over the surface of the potato pastry base, then top with 1 red onion, thinly sliced, and 1 seeded and thinly sliced red or yellow pepper. Drain 2 cans of sardines in olive oil, about 120 g each, and flake into large pieces. Scatter over the tart together with 6 thinly sliced midget gherkins. Bake as in the main recipe.

Plus points

• Potatoes are a classic source of starchy carbohydrate for everyday meals. Their value as a nutritious and satisfying food was appreciated during the Second World War when the Ministry of Food made sure that they did not become rationed.

• Processed tomatoes in passata contain a high amount of lycopene, a red carotenoid pigment that helps to protect against heart disease and some forms of cancer.

• Chorizo is quite high in fat, but as the paprika-flavoured oil oozes out on cooking, no extra oil need be added to the pan for glazing the shallots.

Yorkshire mince popovers

Yorkshire pudding is a favourite accompaniment to a Sunday roast, but why not enjoy it midweek too, as a main dish? Here it is baked in individual tins, with a savoury pork and vegetable filling. Serve with mashed potatoes mixed with lightly cooked shredded Brussels sprouts for a delicious, well-balanced meal.

Serves 4 (makes 12 popovers)

Batter

125 g (4½ oz) plain flour
2 eggs, lightly beaten
½ tsp sweet paprika
300 ml (10 fl oz) semi-skimmed milk

Pork filling

1 tbsp extra virgin olive oil
300 g (10½ oz) lean minced pork
1 small onion, finely chopped
1 small leek, finely chopped
1 carrot, finely chopped
1 tbsp tomato purée
1 tsp sweet chilli sauce
4 tbsp vegetable stock
1 tbsp chopped parsley
salt and pepper

Preparation time: 45 minutes
Cooking time: 30–35 minutes

Each serving provides

kcal 322, **protein** 26.5 g, **fat** 11 g (of which saturated fat 2 g), **carbohydrate** 32 g (of which sugars 8 g), **fibre** 2 g

✓✓✓	A
✓✓	B₁₂
✓	B₁, B₂, B₆, C, E, folate, niacin, calcium, copper, iron, potassium, zinc

1 First make the batter. Sift the flour into a bowl and add the eggs, paprika, and salt and pepper to taste. Gradually whisk in the milk to make a smooth batter. Leave to stand while making the filling.

2 Heat the oil in a heavy non-stick frying pan. Add the pork and fry over a moderate heat for 5 minutes or until browned, stirring with a wooden spoon to break up the clumps of meat.

3 Remove the pork with a draining spoon and set aside on a plate. Turn down the heat, then add the onion, leek and carrot to the pan. Cook gently for 5 minutes, stirring frequently, until soft and golden. Stir in the tomato purée, chilli sauce and stock. Return the pork to the pan. Cook gently for a further 15 minutes, stirring frequently.

4 Preheat the oven to 220°C (425°F, gas mark 7). Remove the pork mixture from the heat, and stir in the parsley and salt and pepper to taste.

5 Lightly oil 12 non-stick muffin tins that are 7.5 cm (3 in) across and 3 cm (1¼ in) deep. Put them into the oven to heat for 4 minutes.

6 Stir the batter, then transfer it to a jug to make it easier to pour. Divide the batter among the tins so they are half full. Spoon the pork filling into the centre, piling it up.

7 Bake for 30–35 minutes or until the puddings are well risen and golden brown. Carefully turn out the puddings onto 4 plates and serve immediately.

Plus points

• Lean pork is an excellent source of protein, iron and zinc. Combining vegetables with the meat and batter in this dish provides a healthy family meal.

• Though eggs have received a 'bad press' because of their cholesterol content, this is unfair. For most people, eating foods that are high in cholesterol has little effect on blood cholesterol levels.

• Milk is an important source of vitamin B₂ in the diet. As this vitamin is easily destroyed by ultraviolet light, bottles of milk should not be left exposed to sunlight on the doorstep.

Some more ideas

- Instead of sweet paprika, flavour the batter with 2 tsp wholegrain mustard.
- The batter can be made in a food processor. Simply place all the ingredients in the bowl and mix together.
- To make venison toad-in-the-hole, make the batter as in the main recipe, but adding 2 tbsp chopped fresh herbs (such as parsley, chives or marjoram) in place of the paprika. Spread out 8 venison sausages, about 300 g (10½ oz) in total, in a lightly greased 22 x 30 cm (8½ x 12 in) roasting tin or baking dish. Bake in a preheated 220°C (425°F, gas mark 7) oven for 10 minutes. Pour over the batter and bake for 10 minutes, then reduce the oven temperature to 200°C (400°F, gas mark 6). Bake for a further 20–25 minutes or until the batter is well risen and golden. Serve straight from the dish, with mashed potatoes and swede plus some seasonal greens.

Smoked haddock and potato pie

Fish pie is usually popular with children, who may not otherwise be keen on fish. In this version, leek and watercress are added to boost the vitamin value, and sliced potato and cheese make an appealing topping. Try it with roasted tomatoes on the vine, cooked for about 15 minutes alongside the pie, and steamed broccoli.

Serves 6

750 ml (1¼ pints) plus 3 tbsp semi-skimmed milk

500 g (1 lb 2 oz) smoked haddock fillets

1 bay leaf

1 large leek, halved lengthways and sliced

550 g (1¼ lb) potatoes, peeled and cut into 5 mm (¼ in) thick slices

3 tbsp cornflour

85 g (3 oz) watercress, thick stalks removed

50 g (1¾ oz) mature Cheddar cheese, coarsely grated

salt and pepper

chopped parsley to garnish

Preparation time: 40 minutes
Cooking time: 25–30 minutes

Each serving provides

kcal 271, **protein** 25 g, **fat** 6 g (of which saturated fat 3 g), **carbohydrate** 32 g (of which sugars 7 g), **fibre** 2 g

✓✓✓	B₁₂, iodine
✓✓	A, B₆, C, niacin, calcium, potassium, selenium
✓	B₁, B₂, folate, copper, zinc

1 Pour the 750 ml (1¼ pints) milk into a wide frying pan. Add the haddock and bay leaf. Bring to a gentle simmer, then cover and cook for about 5 minutes or until the haddock is just cooked.

2 Lift out the fish with a draining spoon and leave to cool slightly, then peel off the skin and break the flesh into large flakes. Set aside. Strain the milk and reserve 600 ml (1 pint), as well as the bay leaf.

3 Put the leek in the frying pan and add the reserved milk and bay leaf. Cover and simmer for 10 minutes or until the leek is tender.

4 Meanwhile, cook the potatoes in a saucepan of boiling water for about 8 minutes or until they are just tender but not breaking up. Drain. Preheat the oven to 190°C (375°F, gas mark 5).

5 Remove the bay leaf from the leeks and discard. Mix the cornflour with the remaining 3 tbsp cold milk to make a smooth paste. Add to the leek mixture and cook gently, stirring, until slightly thickened.

6 Take the pan from the heat and stir in the watercress, which will wilt. Season with salt and pepper to taste. Add the flaked haddock, folding it in gently. Transfer the mixture to a 2 litre (3½ pint) pie dish.

7 Arrange the potato slices on top of the fish mixture, overlapping them slightly. Sprinkle with the cheese, and season with salt and pepper to taste. Bake for 25–30 minutes or until the fish filling is bubbling and the potatoes are turning golden.

8 Sprinkle the top of the pie with parsley and allow to stand for about 5 minutes before serving.

Plus points

• Smoked haddock is an excellent source of iodine and provides useful amounts of vitamin B₆ and potassium. Undyed smoked haddock is now widely available as an alternative to the vibrant yellow-dyed version, which may cause a reaction in susceptible people.

• Potatoes do not contain as much vitamin C as many other vegetables, but they are a valuable source of this vitamin because they are eaten so frequently and in such large amounts.

• Watercress, like other dark green leafy vegetables, is an excellent source of many of the antioxidant nutrients, including beta-carotene, vitamin C and vitamin E.

Some more ideas

• Reduce the amount of smoked haddock to 400 g (14 oz), and add 2 chopped hard-boiled eggs to the fish filling at the end of step 6.

• Use 2 sliced leeks. Omit the watercress and instead, in step 4, add 125 g (4½ oz) baby spinach leaves to the potato slices for the last 1–2 minutes of their cooking time. Drain well. Make a layer of the potatoes and spinach on the bottom of the pie dish. Spoon the hot fish and leek sauce over the top, sprinkle with the cheese and grill under a moderate heat for 5–10 minutes or until bubbling and golden.

• For a smoked haddock, pepper and fennel pie, cook 1 seeded and chopped red pepper, 1 small chopped onion and 2 chopped garlic cloves in 1 tbsp extra virgin olive oil in a large frying pan until the onion is soft. Add 250 g (8½ oz) thinly sliced bulb fennel and cook for a further 5 minutes, stirring occasionally. Stir in 1 can chopped tomatoes, about 400 g, with the juice, and season to taste. Cover and simmer for 25 minutes or until the fennel is tender. Meanwhile, cut the potatoes into chunks instead of slices and cook for 10 minutes or until tender. Pour the pepper and fennel sauce into the pie dish. Lay the skinned smoked haddock fillets on the top (cut to fit if necessary) and scatter over the drained potatoes. Sprinkle with ¼ tsp crushed dried chillies and 30 g (1 oz) freshly grated Parmesan cheese. Bake for about 20 minutes or until golden and bubbling.

Cheddar and broccoli strata

Based on an old-fashioned English recipe, but with an American influence, this satisfying savoury pudding is made up of layers of bread and vegetables with a cheesy egg custard poured over. Served with a quick home-made tomato sauce, it is a tasty and nutritious dish. A leafy salad could be served alongside.

Serves 6

15 g (½ oz) butter

4 shallots, finely chopped

250 g (8½ oz) broccoli, cut into small florets

170 g (6 oz) fine green beans, halved

1 can sweetcorn kernels, about 200 g, drained

9 thick slices of white bread, about 400 g (14 oz) in total, crusts removed and slices cut in half

4 eggs

600 ml (1 pint) semi-skimmed milk

2 tbsp snipped fresh chives

2 tbsp chopped parsley

85 g (3 oz) mature Cheddar cheese, grated

salt and pepper

Tomato sauce

1 tbsp extra virgin olive oil

1 red onion, finely chopped

2 garlic cloves, crushed

2 cans chopped tomatoes with herbs, about 400 g each

2 tbsp tomato purée

Preparation time: 30 minutes, plus 30 minutes standing

Cooking time: 1 hour

1 Melt the butter in a frying pan, add the shallots and cook gently for about 7 minutes or until softened. Meanwhile, cook the broccoli and green beans in a saucepan of boiling water for 4 minutes or until just tender. Drain well, then stir into the shallots together with the sweetcorn. Season to taste.

2 Arrange 6 of the halved bread slices side by side in a lightly greased, deep ovenproof dish. Top with half of the broccoli mixture. Repeat the layers of bread and broccoli mixture, then finish with a layer of bread.

3 Whisk together the eggs, milk, chives and parsley, and season with salt and pepper to taste. Pour over the layered bread and vegetables, and sprinkle the cheese on top. Set aside for 30 minutes, to allow the bread to soak up some of the liquid. Preheat the oven to 180°C (350°F, gas mark 4).

4 Meanwhile, make the tomato sauce. Heat the oil in a saucepan, add the onion and garlic, and cook over a moderate heat for 5 minutes. Stir in the tomatoes, with their juice, and the tomato purée. Bring to the boil, then reduce the heat, cover and simmer for 15 minutes. Uncover the pan, increase the heat slightly and cook for a further 5–10 minutes, stirring occasionally, until the sauce has thickened slightly.

5 Bake the pudding for 1 hour or until set, puffy and golden brown. Just before the cooking time is up, warm the sauce gently. Spoon the strata onto hot serving plates and serve with the tomato sauce.

Plus points

• Cheddar cheese is a good source of protein and an excellent source of calcium. It has a high fat content, but by choosing a mature Cheddar, less can be used while still making a valuable contribution to the flavour and nutritional value of the recipe.

• Sweetcorn provides useful amounts of dietary fibre, which helps to keep the digestive system in good working order.

Each serving provides

kcal 439, **protein** 23 g, **fat** 17 g (of which saturated fat 7 g), **carbohydrate** 53 g (of which sugars 16 g), **fibre** 5 g

✓✓✓	A, B₁₂, C, calcium
✓✓	B₁, B₂, E, folate, niacin, copper, iron, potassium, selenium, zinc
✓	B₆

simple family meals

Some more ideas

- Replace the shallots with 1–2 sliced leeks.
- Flavour the egg custard with chopped fresh oregano or marjoram instead of chives.
- For a higher fibre dish, use wholemeal bread.
- Use Double Gloucester or Lancashire cheese instead of Cheddar.

- To make a sausage and courgette strata, grill 4 good-quality, high-meat-content herby pork sausages. Meanwhile, cook 1 finely chopped onion and 3 sliced courgettes in the butter for 8–10 minutes or until tender. Slice the grilled sausages and mix with the vegetables. Cut the bread into cubes rather than slices. Layer the bread cubes and sausage mixture in the ovenproof dish. Make the egg custard as in the main recipe, but flavour with 1 tbsp chopped fresh rosemary instead of chives and parsley. Omit the cheese. Leave to soak, then bake. Serve with the tomato sauce, and vegetables such as baby carrots and peas.

Beef and chestnut suetcrust pie

This is a warming dish for the cold weather months, rich with lean beef, celeriac, chestnuts and shallots. The suetcrust pastry lid is flavoured with herbs, and breadcrumbs are added for a light, crumbly texture so the pie is not heavy to eat. For extra vitamins serve with lightly cooked spinach.

Serves 4

1 quantity Herbed suetcrust pastry (see Some more ideas, page 24), made with breadcrumbs replacing 30 g (1 oz) of the flour

Beef and chestnut filling

12 small shallots

1 tbsp extra virgin olive oil

300 g (10½ oz) lean braising steak, trimmed of fat and cut into 2.5 cm (1 in) cubes

400 g (14 oz) celeriac, finely diced

360 ml (12 fl oz) beef or vegetable stock

1 tbsp redcurrant jelly

200 g (7 oz) vacuum-packed, peeled whole chestnuts

1 tbsp plain flour

15 g (½ oz) butter, softened

salt and pepper

Preparation time: 1½ hours (including making the pastry)

Cooking time: 30–35 minutes

Each serving provides

kcal 502, **protein** 23 g, **fat** 24 g (of which saturated fat 11 g), **carbohydrate** 52 g (of which sugars 11 g), **fibre** 7 g

✓✓✓	B₁₂, zinc
✓✓	B₁, B₆, C, niacin, calcium, copper, iron, potassium
✓	B₆, E, folate, selenium

1 To make the filling, place the shallots in a heatproof bowl, pour over boiling water to cover and leave for 5 minutes. Drain and, when cool enough to handle, peel the shallots.

2 Heat the oil in a heavy-based pan or flameproof casserole, add the beef and cook over a moderate heat for 4–5 minutes or until browned all over. Remove from the pan to a plate using a draining spoon.

3 Add the shallots to the pan and cook for 4 minutes or until lightly browned. Add the celeriac and cook, stirring, for 1 minute, then return the beef to the pan. Stir in the stock and redcurrant jelly. Bring to the boil, then reduce the heat and simmer gently for 45 minutes or until the beef is tender, stirring frequently.

4 Using a draining spoon, transfer the beef and vegetables to a 1.2 litre (2 pint) pie dish. Stir in the chestnuts. Set aside.

5 Blend the flour with the butter to make a paste (beurre manié). Stir the paste, a little at a time, into the cooking liquid in the pan and simmer, stirring constantly, until the liquid thickens. Season with salt and pepper to taste, then pour this sauce over the beef mixture in the pie dish. Leave to cool while preparing the suetcrust lid.

6 Preheat the oven to 180°C (350°F, gas mark 4). Roll out the suetcrust dough on a lightly floured work surface to a round or oval to fit the top of the pie dish. Dampen the rim of the dish with water, then lay the dough gently over the top. Press firmly to the rim of the dish to seal. Use a fork to make a decorative edge.

7 Cut 3 small slits in the centre of the pastry lid, to allow steam to escape, then bake for 30–35 minutes or until golden brown. Serve hot.

Plus points

• Beef is an excellent source of protein and iron. Iron from red meat is absorbed by the body much more efficiently than iron from vegetable sources.

• Chestnuts have a higher starchy carbohydrate content and a much lower fat content than other nuts. As a result they are also lower in calories.

• Suet is the fat from around lamb's or beef kidneys, which has been shredded and floured. It contains less saturated fat and more monounsaturated fat than butter.

simple family meals

Another idea

- For a minced beef and lentil suetcrust pie, cook 200 g (7 oz) lean minced beef, without any added fat, over a moderate heat until well browned. Add 1 large onion, 3 carrots and 3 celery sticks, all finely chopped, and cook, stirring frequently, for a further 5 minutes or until softened. Stir in 1 can chopped tomatoes, about 400 g, with the juice, 100 g (3½ oz) split red lentils, 360 ml (12 fl oz) beef or vegetable stock and 1 tbsp Worcestershire sauce. Bring to the boil, then simmer gently for 40 minutes, stirring frequently, until thick. Season with salt and pepper to taste. Cool, then pour into the pie dish. Make the suetcrust pastry dough with breadcrumbs, as for the main recipe, but instead of herbs flavour with 1 tbsp wholegrain mustard added to the water. Use the dough to cover the pie and bake as in the main recipe. This is delicious with steamed spring greens and carrots.

Colcannon chicken and apple pie

Colcannon is a simple, warming Irish potato dish, like bubble and squeak, combining mashed potatoes with shredded cooked cabbage and chopped spring onions. Here it is used as a lovely pie topping for chicken cooked in cider with sliced apples and carrots. The pie is a well-balanced meal in itself, needing no accompaniments.

Serves 4

1 tbsp sunflower oil

1 large onion, sliced

450 g (1 lb) skinless boneless chicken breasts (fillets), cut into chunks

3 carrots, thickly sliced

240 ml (8 fl oz) chicken stock

240 ml (8 fl oz) dry cider

1 tsp wholegrain mustard

1 tbsp chopped fresh tarragon or 1 tsp dried tarragon

2 Cox's apples, thickly sliced

1 tbsp cornflour

salt and pepper

Colcannon topping

700 g (1 lb 9 oz) floury potatoes, peeled and cut into large chunks

200 g (7 oz) Savoy cabbage, shredded

4 tbsp semi-skimmed milk

25 g (scant 1 oz) butter

4 spring onions, finely chopped

Preparation and cooking time: 1¼ hours

Each serving provides

kcal 464, **protein** 34 g, **fat** 10 g (of which saturated fat 4 g), **carbohydrate** 60 g (of which sugars 22 g), **fibre** 8 g

✓✓✓	A, B$_6$, C, niacin
✓✓	B$_1$, E, folate, copper, potassium, selenium, zinc
✓	B$_2$, calcium, iron

1 Heat the oil in a large, deep, non-stick frying pan. Add the onion and cook over a low heat for 5 minutes or until softened.

2 Add the chicken to the pan and cook over a moderate heat, stirring occasionally, for 5 minutes or until it is no longer pink. Stir in the carrots.

3 Combine the stock, cider, mustard and tarragon, and pour into the pan. Bring to the boil, then reduce the heat, cover and cook gently for 10 minutes. Stir in the apples and cook, covered, for a further 10 minutes or until the chicken and carrots are tender, and the apples have softened but are still holding their shape.

4 Meanwhile, cook the potatoes in a saucepan of boiling water for about 15 minutes or until tender. Cook the cabbage in a separate pan of boiling water for 4–5 minutes or until just tender but not soft; drain well.

5 Drain the potatoes and return them to the pan. Add the milk and butter, and mash until smooth. Stir in the cabbage and spring onions, and season with salt and pepper to taste. Cover to keep warm.

6 Using a draining spoon, transfer the chicken, apples and vegetables to a 1.7 litre (3 pint) ovenproof dish. Set aside. Preheat the grill to high.

7 Mix the cornflour with 1 tbsp cold water, stir into the cooking liquid in the frying pan and bring to the boil, stirring until thickened. Season with salt and pepper to taste, then pour over the chicken mixture.

8 Pile the potato and cabbage topping over the chicken mixture, spreading it evenly to cover. Place under the grill and cook for 4–5 minutes or until golden brown. Serve immediately.

Plus points

• Savoy cabbage contains flavonoids that are believed to help suppress cancer-causing cells. It also contains other nutrients with protective properties, such as vitamins C and E.

• Adding a green vegetable such as cabbage to a mashed potato topping is a tasty and clever way of increasing the vegetable content of a meal. It will also be appealing to children who may not always be fond of vegetables like cabbage when they are served separately.

Some more ideas

• Replace the cider with pressed apple juice.

• Instead of cabbage and spring onions, use leeks in the potato topping. Cook 2 sliced leeks in the butter until tender. Mash the potatoes with the milk, then mix in the buttery leeks.

• Make sherried liver topped with minted pea mash. Soften 1 sliced onion in 1 tbsp sunflower oil, then add 400 g (14 oz) lamb's liver, cut into strips and cook for 2–3 minutes. Add 2 sliced courgettes. Combine 250 ml (8½ fl oz) lamb or chicken stock, 2 tbsp medium-dry sherry, the grated zest and juice of 1 orange, and 1 tbsp tomato purée, and pour over the liver mixture. Bring to the boil, then reduce the heat and cook gently for 10 minutes. Transfer the liver and vegetables to the ovenproof dish. Thicken the liquid with 1 tbsp cornflour as in the main recipe, season and pour into the dish. For the topping, cook the potatoes for 10 minutes, then add 200 g (7 oz) mint-flavoured frozen peas. Bring back to the boil and cook for a further 5 minutes or until the potatoes are tender. Drain and crush roughly with a fork, mixing in the milk, butter and 2 tbsp snipped fresh chives. Spread over the top of the liver mixture and grill as in the main recipe.

Herbed lamb cobbler

A hearty hotpot of lean lamb chunks, leeks, carrots, tomatoes and broccoli with a herbed scone topping is sure to satisfy a hungry family. To complete the meal, serve with lightly steamed green beans or another seasonal green vegetable, to boost the vitamin content of the meal.

Serves 4

1 quantity Herbed scone pastry (see Some more ideas, page 23), made with plain low-fat yogurt instead of milk

1 tbsp semi-skimmed milk

Lamb filling

1 tbsp sunflower oil

450 g (1 lb) boneless leg of lamb, trimmed of fat and cut into bite-sized cubes

450 g (1 lb) leeks, thickly sliced

350 g (12½ oz) carrots, thickly sliced

1 can plum tomatoes, about 400 g

200 ml (7 fl oz) lamb stock

2 tbsp chopped fresh thyme

200 g (7 oz) broccoli, broken into florets

salt and pepper

Preparation time: 45 minutes (including making the pastry)

Cooking time: 20 minutes

Each serving provides

kcal 519, **protein** 34 g, **fat** 19 g (of which saturated fat 5 g), **carbohydrate** 55 g (of which sugars 15 g), **fibre** 8 g

✓✓✓ A, C, E

✓✓ B$_1$, B$_6$, folate, calcium, iron, potassium

✓ niacin, copper, zinc

---

1 To make the filling, heat the oil in a non-stick frying pan, add the lamb and cook for 3–4 minutes, stirring occasionally, until lightly browned. Add the leeks and carrots, and cook, stirring, for 1 minute.

2 Add the tomatoes with their juice, the stock, thyme, and salt and pepper to taste. Bring to the boil, then reduce the heat, cover and simmer gently for 30 minutes or until the lamb is tender.

3 Roll out the scone dough on a lightly floured surface to 1 cm (½ in) thickness. Cut into 12 triangles. Preheat the oven to 220°C (425°F, gas mark 7).

4 Add the broccoli to the lamb stew. and stir in. Cover again, increase the heat slightly and cook for a further 5 minutes.

5 Spoon the lamb stew into a 2 litre (3½ pint) ovenproof dish. Arrange the scone dough triangles on top, overlapping them slightly. Brush with the milk to glaze. Bake for 20 minutes or until the scone topping is risen and golden brown. Serve hot.

Another idea

• To make a Hungarian-style turkey cobbler, lightly brown 300 g (10½ oz) skinless boneless turkey breast, cut into bite-sized cubes, in 1 tbsp sunflower oil with 1 thinly sliced onion and 1 crushed garlic clove. Stir in 300 g (10½ oz) peeled, diced potatoes, 200 ml (7 fl oz) chicken stock, 1 can chopped tomatoes, about 400 g, with the juice, and 1 tbsp paprika. Bring to the boil, then cover and simmer gently for 20 minutes. Stir in 300 g (10½ oz) fresh shelled or frozen broad beans. Bring back to the boil, then simmer, covered, for about 5 minutes. For the scone topping, replace the herbs with 1 tbsp caraway seeds, and cut the dough into 12 rounds. Transfer the turkey stew to an ovenproof dish, arrange the scone rounds on top and glaze with milk. Bake as in the main recipe.

Plus points

• Lamb has a reputation for being a fatty meat, but changes in breeding, feeding and butchery techniques have reduced the fat content considerably.

• Carrots are rich in beta-carotene, which helps to protect cells against damage by free radicals. Older, darker carrots contain more beta-carotene than young, pale ones.

Aztec chicken pie

Teenagers especially will love this unusual pie, which layers flour tortillas with diced chicken and red kidney beans in a spicy tomato, sweetcorn and pepper sauce. Serve with a green salad and a side dish of diced avocado sprinkled with lime juice, for a meal with an exciting Mexican flavour.

Serves 6

6 large flour tortillas (wraps)
150 g (5½ oz) plain low-fat yogurt
90 ml (3 fl oz) soured cream
75 g (2½ oz) mature Cheddar cheese, finely grated

Mexican chicken filling

2 tbsp extra virgin olive oil
1 large Spanish onion, chopped
2 garlic cloves, crushed
1 green pepper, seeded and chopped
200 g (7 oz) baby corn, chopped
1 fresh red chilli, seeded and chopped
2 cans chopped tomatoes, about 400 g each
1 tsp ground coriander
1 tsp ground cumin
1 tsp caster sugar
1 good-quality chicken stock cube or 1 tsp chicken bouillon powder
300 g (10½ oz) cooked skinless, boneless chicken breast (fillet), diced
1 can red kidney beans, about 410 g, drained and rinsed
6 tbsp chopped fresh coriander
salt and pepper

Preparation time: 35–40 minutes
Cooking time: 25 minutes

1 First make the filling. Heat the oil in a large pan, add the onion and cook for 10 minutes or until softened. Stir in the garlic, green pepper, corn and chilli, and cook for 5 more minutes.

2 Add the tomatoes with their juice, the ground coriander, cumin, sugar and stock cube or bouillon. Season with salt and pepper to taste, and stir well. Bring to the boil, then reduce the heat and simmer for 10 minutes.

3 Stir in the chicken, beans and half the fresh coriander. Heat through gently for 5 minutes. Preheat the oven to 200°C (400°F, gas mark 6).

4 Lightly oil a large china flan dish, measuring about 28 cm (11 in) in diameter and 5 cm (2 in) deep. Place a tortilla on the bottom and spoon over one-fifth of the filling. Cover with a second tortilla, then spread over another fifth of the filling. Continue layering, finishing with the last tortilla on top. The stack will be slightly higher than the side of the dish.

5 Mix the yogurt with the soured cream, 50 g (1¾ oz) of the cheese and 2 tbsp of the remaining coriander. Spoon over the top of the pie. Sprinkle with the remaining cheese. Bake for 25 minutes or until the top is golden. Sprinkle with the rest of the coriander and serve hot, cut into wedges.

Plus points

• Tortillas, whether made from masa harina, a type of cornmeal, or wheat, are a good source of starchy carbohydrates.

• There is little nutritional difference between canned red kidney beans and cooked dried ones, and canned beans are certainly a lot more convenient.

• Chicken is an excellent source of protein and a good source of many of the B vitamins, particularly B_1 and niacin. Eaten without the skin, it is low in fat and the fat that is present in the meat is mainly the more beneficial unsaturated type.

Each serving provides

kcal 517, **protein** 29 g, **fat** 13 g (of which saturated fat 5.5 g), **carbohydrate** 75 g (of which sugars 17 g), **fibre** 7.5 g

✓✓✓	C, niacin
✓✓	A, B_1, B_6, E, folate, calcium, copper, potassium, zinc
✓	B_2, iron, selenium

simple family meals

Some more ideas

• As an alternative topping, mix 200 g (7 oz) fromage frais with 85 g (3 oz) finely grated Manchego cheese and the 2 tbsp chopped fresh coriander.

• To make a borlotti bean tortilla pie, soften the onion, then add the crushed garlic, 1 seeded and chopped yellow pepper, 250 g (8½ oz) chopped courgettes and 500 g (1 lb 2 oz) chopped bulb fennel. Cook for 5 minutes, then stir in the tomatoes, ground coriander, sugar, stock cube or bouillon and seasoning to taste.

Simmer for 10 minutes. Add 2 cans borlotti beans, about 410 g each, drained and rinsed, and heat through. Layer the bean mixture with the flour tortillas, top with the yogurt mixture or the fromage frais mixture and bake as in the main recipe.

Chunky vegetable crumble

A tasty mixture of root vegetables and creamy butter beans topped with a savoury cheese crumble makes a nourishing vegetarian dish. Sunflower seeds are added to the crumble for added texture and extra protein.

Serves 4

1 tbsp sunflower oil

1 onion, sliced

2 garlic cloves, crushed

3 carrots, cut into 2 cm (¾ in) chunks

2 parsnips, cut into 2 cm (¾ in) chunks

250 g (8½ oz) baby turnips, quartered

350 g (12½ oz) waxy new potatoes, scrubbed and cut into 2 cm (¾ in) chunks

450 ml (15 fl oz) vegetable stock

generous dash of Worcestershire sauce

1 tbsp tomato purée

2 bay leaves

1 can butter beans, about 410 g, drained and rinsed

3 tbsp chopped parsley

salt and pepper

Sunflower seed crumble topping

85 g (3 oz) wholemeal flour

30 g (1 oz) cool butter, diced

75 g (2½ oz) mature Cheddar cheese, coarsely grated

30 g (1 oz) sunflower seeds

Preparation time: 40 minutes

Cooking time: 20 minutes

1 Heat the oil in a large saucepan, add the onion and cook gently for 10 minutes or until softened. Add the garlic and cook for 1 more minute.

2 Add the carrots, parsnips, turnips and potatoes. Stir in the stock, Worcestershire sauce, tomato purée and bay leaves. Bring to the boil, then reduce the heat, cover and simmer for 20 minutes, stirring occasionally.

3 Meanwhile, make the crumble topping. Put the flour in a bowl and rub in the butter. Sprinkle over 1½ tbsp cold water and mix together with a fork to make large crumbs. Stir in the cheese and sunflower seeds. Set aside.

4 Preheat the oven to 190°C (375°F, gas mark 5). Stir the butter beans into the vegetables and cook for a further 5–7 minutes or until the vegetables are just tender. Remove and discard the bay leaves.

5 Remove a large ladleful of the vegetables and stock, and mash until smooth or purée in a blender or processor. Stir the purée into the vegetable mixture in the pan to thicken it slightly. Stir in the parsley, and season with salt and pepper to taste.

6 Spoon the vegetable mixture into a lightly greased 1.7 litre (3 pint) ovenproof dish. Sprinkle the crumble mixture evenly over the top. Bake for 20 minutes or until golden brown.

Plus points

• Together, parsnips and turnips provide fibre, B vitamins and potassium and are a surprisingly useful source of vitamin C.

• New potatoes, scrubbed but not peeled, have one-third more dietary fibre than peeled potatoes. The nutrients found just under the skin will also be preserved.

• Sunflower seeds are rich in vitamin E. They also offer vitamin B_1, iron and phosphorus.

Each serving provides Ⓥ

kcal 465, **protein** 17 g, **fat** 21 g (of which saturated fat 9 g), **carbohydrate** 55.5 g (of which sugars 16 g), **fibre** 12.5 g

✓✓✓	A, C, E, copper
✓✓	B_1, B_6, folate, niacin, calcium, potassium, selenium, zinc
✓	iron

simple family meals

74

Some more ideas

- Replace 1 of the carrots with 250 g (8½ oz) quartered kohlrabi.
- For an oaty vegetable crumble, gently cook 1 large sliced onion in 1 tbsp extra virgin olive oil for 10 minutes or until soft. Add 2 crushed garlic cloves, then stir in 1 aubergine, about 200 g (7 oz), 1 acorn squash, about 500 g

(1 lb 2 oz) and 300 g (10½ oz) courgettes, all cut into 2 cm (¾ in) chunks. Cook, stirring, for 5 minutes. Add 400 ml (14 fl oz) vegetable stock, 30 g (1 oz) chopped sun-dried tomatoes, 2 tsp chopped fresh thyme and seasoning to taste. Cover and simmer for 15–20 minutes or until all the vegetables are tender. Stir in 1 can of cannellini beans, about 410 g, drained and

rinsed. Remove a large ladleful of the mixture, containing mostly squash, tomatoes and beans, and mash or purée, then return to the pan to thicken the mixture. For the crumble, use 30 g (1 oz) freshly grated Parmesan cheese instead of Cheddar, and replace the sunflower seeds with 30 g (1 oz) jumbo oats. Bake as in the main recipe.

Pizza tart with cherry tomatoes

A Parmesan-flavoured pizza dough makes a delicious case for a ricotta cheese and herb filling topped with sweet cherry tomatoes and black olives. Serve with a salad of mixed leaves and poppy, pumpkin and sunflower seeds, toasted to bring out their flavour, for a tempting and nutritious meal.

Serves 4

Parmesan pizza dough

170 g (6 oz) strong white (bread) flour

½ tsp easy-blend dried yeast

30 g (1 oz) Parmesan cheese, freshly grated

120 ml (4 fl oz) tepid water

2 tbsp extra virgin olive oil

Ricotta filling

170 g (6 oz) ricotta cheese

2 tsp chopped fresh oregano

1 tbsp chopped parsley

250 g (8½ oz) cherry tomatoes, halved

50 g (1¾ oz) stoned black olives

2 tbsp balsamic vinegar

1 small sprig of fresh rosemary

1 garlic clove, crushed

salt and pepper

Leafy salad with mixed seeds

50 g (1¾ oz) pumpkin seeds

50 g (1¾ oz) sunflower seeds

2 tsp poppy seeds

1 tsp soy sauce

2 tsp sunflower oil

1 tsp walnut oil

1 tsp cider vinegar

150 g (5½ oz) mixed salad leaves, such as baby spinach, rocket and Oak Leaf lettuce

Preparation time: 35–40 minutes, plus
   1 hour rising

Cooking time: 15–20 minutes

1 To make the dough, sift the flour and ½ tsp salt into a bowl, and stir in the yeast and Parmesan cheese. Make a well in the centre. Add the water and 1 tbsp of the oil, and mix to form a dough. Add a bit more water if needed.

2 Turn out onto a lightly floured surface and knead for 10 minutes or until smooth and elastic. Return the dough to the bowl, cover with cling film and leave in a warm place to rise for about 1 hour or until doubled in size.

3 Preheat the oven to 220°C (425°F, gas mark 7) and place a baking sheet inside to heat. Knock back the dough, then turn it out onto the floured surface and knead briefly. Roll out to a 30 cm (12 in) round about 5 mm (¼ in) thick. Use to line a lightly oiled, loose-bottomed, shallow 25 cm (10 in) tart tin, leaving the edges ragged and slightly hanging over the edge of the tin.

4 Mix the ricotta with the oregano and parsley, and season with salt and pepper to taste. Spread evenly in the dough case. Arrange the tomatoes, cut side up, and the olives on top.

5 Gently heat the balsamic vinegar with the remaining 1 tbsp olive oil, the rosemary and garlic in a small pan. Bubble for 1–2 minutes or until it has reduced a little, then drizzle over the tomatoes and olives.

6 Place the tart tin on the preheated baking sheet. Bake for 15–20 minutes or until the case is crisp and golden brown and the tomatoes are slightly caramelised.

7 Meanwhile, make the salad. In a small non-stick frying pan, toast the pumpkin, sunflower and poppy seeds over a moderate heat for 2–3 minutes, turning frequently. Sprinkle over the soy sauce and toss together. The seeds will stick together initially, but will separate as the mixture dries. Remove from the heat.

8 Whisk together the sunflower and walnut oils, vinegar and seasoning to taste in a salad bowl. Add the salad leaves, sprinkle with the toasted seeds and toss together.

9 Remove the tart from the tin and cut it into 4 wedges. Serve hot, with the salad.

Each serving (with salad) provides
kcal 490, **protein** 18 g, **fat** 30 g (of which saturated fat 7.5 g), **carbohydrate** 41 g (of which sugars 4 g), **fibre** 4 g

✓✓✓	A, E, calcium, copper
✓✓	B₁, C, niacin, iron, zinc
✓	B₂, folate, potassium, selenium

simple family meals

Some more ideas

• Use baby plum tomatoes instead of cherry tomatoes.

• Make a prawn and mushroom pizza tart. While the dough is rising, gently cook 300 g (10½ oz) sliced mixed mushrooms in 1 tbsp extra virgin olive oil until just tender. Using a draining spoon, transfer the mushrooms to a bowl and mix with 150 g (5½ oz) peeled raw prawns, 4 skinned, chopped and seeded tomatoes, 1 can of anchovies, about 50 g, drained and chopped, 1 tbsp drained capers, and salt and pepper to taste. Spoon into the pizza dough case and bake as in the main recipe. Serve with a salad of baby plum tomatoes, cucumber and spring onions.

Plus point

• Tomatoes are an excellent source of vitamin C. This important nutrient is found mainly in the jellylike substance surrounding the tomato seeds.

Cheesy rice with asparagus

This is an easy and attractive vegetarian dish. The rice is cooked in stock, then mixed with peas, asparagus and cheese, and baked in individual dishes. Choose a tangy Cheddar cheese for maximum flavour – a little will go a long way. A tomato and herb salad is a perfect accompaniment for these savoury rice puddings.

Serves 4

1 tbsp melted butter

2 tbsp dried breadcrumbs

300 g (10½ oz) long-grain or basmati rice

600 ml (1 pint) vegetable stock

150 g (5½ oz) frozen peas

150 g (5½ oz) asparagus, cut into 5 cm (2 in) pieces

3 eggs

100 g (3½ oz) mature Cheddar cheese, grated

¼ tsp crushed dried chillies

salt and pepper

Preparation time: 25 minutes

Cooking time: 20 minutes

Each serving provides Ⓥ

kcal 508, **protein** 22 g, **fat** 16 g (of which saturated fat 8 g), **carbohydrate** 70 g (of which sugars 2 g), **fibre** 3 g

✓✓✓	B₁₂
✓✓	A, folate, calcium, zinc
✓	B₁, B₂, C, E, niacin, copper, iron, selenium

1 First prepare 4 individual baking dishes that are 360 ml (12 fl oz) capacity. Lightly grease with the melted butter, then dust with the breadcrumbs to coat the bottom and sides. Preheat the oven to 190°C (375°F, gas mark 5).

2 Place the rice in a medium-sized saucepan, pour over the stock and bring to the boil. Reduce the heat, cover tightly and simmer gently for 5 minutes, without stirring.

3 Uncover the pan and stir in the peas and asparagus. Bring back to the boil, then reduce the heat and simmer gently, covered, for a further 5 minutes.

4 Remove the pan from the heat. Stir, then cover again and leave the rice and vegetables to stand undisturbed for 5–7 minutes.

5 Combine the eggs and cheese in a mixing bowl. Add the chilli flakes, and salt and pepper to taste. Mix with a fork until well blended. Add the rice mixture and stir gently until thoroughly combined.

6 Divide the rice mixture evenly among the 4 prepared dishes. Set them on a baking sheet and bake for 20 minutes or until set and the tops are golden and crisp. Serve hot.

Some more ideas

• Instead of peas, use frozen sweetcorn, frozen broad beans or frozen mixed vegetables.

• To make a pepper and tomato rice bake, cook the rice in 600 ml (1 pint) tomato juice with a dash of Tabasco sauce to taste, rather than stock, omitting the peas and asparagus. While the rice is cooking, gently soften 1 red, 1 yellow and 1 green pepper, all seeded and thinly sliced, with 1 crushed garlic clove in 1 tbsp extra virgin olive oil. Divide the peppers among 4 individual baking dishes, or spread over the bottom of a 1.5 litre (2¾ pint) baking dish, greased and dusted with breadcrumbs. Stir the eggs into the cooked rice with 2 tbsp snipped fresh chives and seasoning to taste (omit the Cheddar cheese). Spoon on top of the peppers, then scatter over 2 tbsp freshly grated Parmesan cheese. Bake as in the main recipe.

Plus points

• Rice is the most important cereal grain in the world. It is a source of protein and most B vitamins as well as starchy carbohydrate.

• Asparagus is a rich source of many of the B vitamins, especially folate. Folate not only helps to prevent birth defects such as spina bifida, if sufficient is consumed in the early stages of pregnancy, it may also help to protect against heart disease.

Ham and corn polenta tart

Soft buttery polenta makes a lovely golden tart case, prettily flecked with green herbs. The filling is an appetising combination of diced ham, broccoli florets, baby corn and spring onions in a mustardy egg custard. Serve warm with a salad such as lightly blanched French beans tossed with sliced courgettes.

Serves 4

Herbed polenta

150 g (5½ oz) instant polenta
600 ml (1 pint) chicken stock
25 g (scant 1 oz) butter, softened
2 tbsp chopped fresh chives
2 tbsp chopped parsley
salt and pepper

Ham and corn filling

250 g (8½ oz) broccoli, cut into small florets
85 g (3 oz) baby corn, halved lengthways
200 g (7 oz) lean cooked ham, diced
3 spring onions, thinly sliced
3 eggs, beaten
240 ml (8 fl oz) semi-skimmed milk
1 tsp Dijon mustard
2 tbsp snipped fresh chives to garnish

Preparation time: 25 minutes, plus 10 minutes cooling
Cooking time: 35–40 minutes

Each serving provides

kcal 369, **protein** 25 g, **fat** 14 g (of which saturated fat 6 g), **carbohydrate** 35.5 g (of which sugars 5 g), **fibre** 5 g

✓✓✓	C
✓✓	A, B$_{12}$, zinc
✓	B$_1$, B$_2$, B$_6$, E, folate, niacin, calcium, iron, potassium, selenium

1 Preheat the oven to 190°C (375°F, gas mark 5). Heat the stock in a large saucepan until boiling, then pour in the polenta in a steady stream, stirring constantly with a wooden spoon to prevent lumps from forming. Cook over a moderate heat, stirring, for about 5 minutes or until thick and smooth, and pulling away from the sides of the pan.

2 Remove from the heat and beat in the butter, chives, parsley, and salt and pepper to taste. Set aside to cool for about 10 minutes.

3 Spoon the polenta into a lightly oiled, straight-sided 25 cm (10 in) loose-bottomed flan tin that is about 4 cm (1½ in) deep. Spread out the polenta with the back of a metal spoon to cover the bottom and sides smoothly and evenly. Set the tin on a baking sheet.

4 To make the filling, cook the broccoli and corn in a saucepan of boiling water for 3 minutes. Drain well and spoon into the polenta case. Scatter over the diced ham and spring onions.

5 Whisk together the eggs, milk, mustard and seasoning to taste. Pour over the ham and vegetables. Bake for 35–40 minutes or until golden brown and just set.

6 To serve, carefully remove the tart from the tin and sprinkle the top with the chives. Serve warm.

Plus points

• Polenta is low in fat and a rich source of starchy carbohydrate. Including it in the diet can help to meet the healthy eating recommendations to increase carbohydrate intake and decrease fat intake.

• Ham is a particularly good source of vitamin B$_1$, essential for the release of energy from carbohydrate foods such as polenta.

• Broccoli is packed with vitamins, including many of the antioxidants as well as vitamin B$_6$, folate and niacin. It is also a good source of phytochemicals, particularly indoles which research suggests may be helpful in protecting against breast cancer.

simple family meals

Some more ideas

- Instead of baby corn, use drained canned sweetcorn or frozen sweetcorn.
- For a vegetarian chickpea and corn polenta tart, cook the polenta in vegetable stock, and replace the ham with 1 can of chickpeas, about 410 g, drained and rinsed.
- Make a bresaola and artichoke polenta pie. Flavour the polenta with 4 tbsp chopped fresh basil in place of the parsley and chives. Cool until firm enough to handle, then press two-thirds over the bottom and sides of a lightly greased 23 cm (9 in) metal pie dish. Arrange 100 g (3½ oz) chopped bresaola (air-dried beef), 2 sliced tomatoes and 1 can of artichoke hearts, about 400 g, drained and halved, in the polenta case. Beat 2 eggs with 120 ml (4 fl oz) semi-skimmed milk and seasoning to taste. Pour into the polenta case. Press out the remaining polenta on a lightly floured surface into a round about 5 mm (¼ in) thick, and cut out twelve 4 cm (1½ in) rounds. Arrange over the filling, slightly overlapping. Brush lightly with 1 tsp extra virgin olive oil and sprinkle with 30 g (1 oz) freshly grated Parmesan cheese. Bake in a preheated 180°C (350°F, gas mark 4) oven for 40 minutes or until golden brown.

Savoury Dishes for Entertaining

Special main-dish pies, tarts and puddings

Here are some impressive dishes to disprove the notion that pies and puddings are not dinner party fare. For example, a spinach and goat's cheese pie with a crisp, scrunched-up filo lid looks really grand, as does a filo 'crown' filled with couscous and prawns. An asparagus tart, with an unusual, light-textured yeasted shortcrust case, is very special too. Guinea fowl cooked with mushrooms in Madeira wine is an unexpectedly luxurious filling for a 'pudding in a basin'. This one has a lovely potato pastry crust too, and is baked rather than steamed.

Scrunch-top filo pie

Spinach and tangy goat's cheese make perfect partners in this impressive-looking Greek-style filo pastry pie. Colourful diced tomatoes and toasted pine nuts in the filling add to the appeal. Serve with boiled new potatoes and a dish of mixed vegetables, such as thinly sliced carrots and courgettes tossed with fresh tarragon leaves.

savoury dishes for entertaining

Serves 4

2 sheets filo pastry, 30 x 50 cm (12 x 20 in)
 each, about 60 g (2¼ oz) in total
1 tbsp sunflower oil

Spinach and goat's cheese filling

30 g (1 oz) pine nuts
675 g (1½ lb) baby spinach leaves, trimmed
 of any large stalks
200 g (7 oz) soft goat's cheese
2 tsp plain flour
2 eggs, lightly beaten
¼ tsp freshly grated nutmeg
4 tomatoes, about 300 g (10½ oz) in total,
 diced
salt and pepper

Preparation time: 25 minutes
Cooking time: 25–30 minutes

Each serving provides

kcal 326, **protein** 18 g, **fat** 21 g (of which
saturated fat 7 g), **carbohydrate** 17 g (of
which sugars 6 g), **fibre** 4.5 g

✓✓✓	A, B₁₂, C, E, folate, calcium
✓✓	B₂, niacin, iron, potassium, zinc
✓	B₁, B₆, copper

1 Preheat the oven to 180°C (350°F, gas mark 4). To make the filling, toast the pine nuts in a large saucepan for 2–3 minutes, stirring frequently, until golden brown. Remove and set aside.

2 Add half the spinach to the saucepan, with just the water used for washing still clinging to the leaves. Cover and cook for 3–4 minutes or until wilted and tender. Tip into a colander to drain while you cook the remaining spinach. Press out excess water, then roughly chop the spinach.

3 Put the cheese in a bowl and sprinkle over the flour, then gradually beat in the eggs. Stir in the spinach, pine nuts and nutmeg, and season with salt and pepper to taste.

4 Spoon half of the spinach mixture into a 1.4 litre (2½ pint) ovenproof dish that is about 5 cm (2 in) deep. Top with the tomatoes, then cover with the remaining spinach mixture.

5 Cut each sheet of filo pastry into eight 12.5 cm (5 in) squares, discarding the excess pastry. Brush the squares with the oil, then crumple them up loosely and place oil side up over the filling. Bake for 25–30 minutes or until the filling is lightly set and the pastry topping is golden brown and crisp. Serve hot.

Some more ideas

• For a lower-fat version, use quark or ricotta cheese instead of goat's cheese.

• To make a squash and cashew nut filo pie, toast 30 g (1 oz) cashew nuts, then coarsely chop. Steam 1 butternut squash, about 600 g (1 lb 5 oz), cut into 1 cm (½ in) cubes, for 6–7 minutes or until just tender. Mix 200 g (7 oz) curd cheese with 2 beaten eggs, then add the squash, cashew nuts, 1 coarsely grated carrot and 25 g (scant 1 oz) pumpkin seeds. Season with salt and pepper to taste and mix well. Spoon into a lightly greased ovenproof dish, top with the scrunched-up filo and bake as in the main recipe.

Plus points

• Spinach is a great source of many of the antioxidants that help to protect against cancer, including vitamins C and E and beta-carotene. The beta-carotene content of spinach is 6 times greater than that of broccoli.

• Pine nuts, also called pine kernels, are a good source of vitamin E and potassium. Though relatively new to many British cooks, husks recovered from Roman camp rubbish tips in the UK suggest that the Romans included pine nuts in their diet.

Mediterranean chickpea pie

Enjoy the taste of the Mediterranean with this vegetarian pie. It's packed with vegetables and chickpeas cooked in red wine with tomatoes and Italian herbs, and is topped with a Parmesan, sun-dried tomato and fresh basil mash. Serve with a seasonal green vegetable, such as Savoy cabbage, for extra vitamins and minerals.

Serves 6

2 tbsp extra virgin olive oil
2 onions, chopped
2 celery sticks, chopped
1 red pepper, seeded and diced
2 garlic cloves, crushed
2 courgettes, sliced
2 cans chickpeas, about 410 g each, drained
    and rinsed
2 cans chopped tomatoes, about 400 g each
2 tbsp sun-dried tomato paste
150 ml (5 fl oz) red wine
2 tsp dried Italian herb seasoning
salt and pepper

Parmesan and tomato mash

1 kg (2¼ lb) potatoes, peeled and cut into
    chunks
4 tbsp semi-skimmed milk
1 egg
50 g (1¾ oz) Parmesan cheese, freshly
    grated
50 g (1¾ oz) sun-dried tomatoes in oil,
    drained and finely chopped
3 tbsp chopped fresh basil

Preparation time: 55 minutes
Cooking time: 25 minutes

1 Heat 1 tbsp of the oil in a large pan, add the onions, celery, red pepper and garlic, and sauté for 5 minutes. Add the courgettes, chickpeas, tomatoes with their juice, tomato paste, wine and dried herbs. Season with salt and pepper to taste and mix well.

2 Bring to the boil, then reduce the heat. Cover the pan and simmer for 20 minutes, stirring occasionally. Uncover the pan, increase the heat and cook for a further 10–15 minutes, stirring occasionally, until the liquid has thickened slightly.

3 Meanwhile, cook the potatoes in a saucepan of boiling water for 15–20 minutes or until tender. Preheat the oven to 200°C (400°F, gas mark 6).

4 Drain the potatoes well, then return to the pan. Add the milk and the remaining 1 tbsp olive oil, and mash until smooth. Beat in the egg, Parmesan cheese, sun-dried tomatoes, chopped basil, and salt and pepper to taste. Mix well.

5 Spoon the vegetable mixture into an ovenproof dish. Top with the Parmesan mash, covering the vegetables completely. Mark the top of the mash decoratively with a fork.

6 Bake the pie for 25 minutes or until the potato topping is nicely browned. Serve hot.

Plus points

- Chickpeas, like other pulses, are a good source of dietary fibre. This is present mainly as the soluble type of fibre, which is helpful in reducing high blood cholesterol levels.
- Courgettes are a good source of the B vitamins niacin and B_6. It is important to eat the skins as this is where the greatest concentration of these nutrients is to be found.
- Celery provides useful amounts of potassium as well as a compound called phthalide, which is believed to help lower high blood pressure.

Each serving provides
kcal 426, **protein** 18 g, **fat** 15 g (of which saturated fat 3.5 g), **carbohydrate** 54 g (of which sugars 12 g), **fibre** 8 g

✓✓✓	A, B_6, C, E, copper
✓✓	B_1, folate, niacin, calcium, iron, potassium, zinc
✓	B_2, B_{12}

savoury dishes for entertaining

Some more ideas

• Use canned cannellini or flageolet beans instead of chickpeas.

• Replace the celery with 2 chopped carrots.

• Add chopped black olives to the mash rather than sun-dried tomatoes.

• If Italian herb seasoning is unavailable, use any combination of dried basil, oregano, parsley, thyme and sage.

• To make a spiced lamb pie, sauté 2 chopped red onions, 1 red and 1 yellow pepper, both seeded and chopped, 2 crushed garlic cloves, and 1–2 seeded and finely chopped fresh red chillies in 1 tbsp extra virgin olive oil for about 5 minutes or until softened. Stir in 2 tsp each ground cumin and coriander, then add 350 g (12½ oz) lean minced lamb and cook for 3–4 minutes or until browned. Add 1 small diced aubergine, 250 g (8½ oz) halved button mushrooms, 1 can chopped tomatoes, about 400 g, with the juice, 2 tbsp tomato purée and 200 ml (7 fl oz) lamb or beef stock or red wine (or a mixture). Cover and simmer for about 45 minutes. For the topping, cook the potatoes, then mash with 1 tbsp extra virgin olive oil and 100 ml (3½ fl oz) semi-skimmed milk. Mix in 3 tbsp chopped fresh coriander and seasoning to taste. Transfer the lamb mixture to an ovenproof dish, cover with the mash and bake as in the main recipe.

Provençale roasted vegetable and feta slice

This colourful tart combines classic flavours of Provence – peppers, courgettes, tomatoes, garlic and fresh herbs – with piquant feta cheese in a crisp, olive oil pastry case. The tart can be served hot or cold, and would be lovely for a summer picnic or alfresco lunch in the garden.

Serves 4

1 quantity Olive oil shortcrust pastry (see Some more ideas, page 22), rested for 30 minutes

Pepper and feta filling

1 large red pepper, seeded and chopped

1 large yellow pepper, seeded and chopped

2 medium courgettes, thickly sliced

1½ tbsp extra virgin olive oil

2 garlic cloves, sliced

few sprigs of fresh thyme

4 plum tomatoes, quartered

150 g (5½ oz) feta cheese, roughly chopped

2 tsp semi-skimmed milk

1 tsp poppy seeds (optional)

salt and pepper

Preparation and cooking time: 1½ hours (including making the pastry), plus 30 minutes resting

---

Each serving provides Ⓥ

kcal 446, **protein** 14 g, **fat** 26 g (of which saturated fat 8 g), **carbohydrate** 42 g (of which sugars 9 g), **fibre** 4 g

✓✓✓	A, C
✓✓	B₁₂, E, calcium
✓	B₁, B₆, folate, niacin, copper, iron, potassium, zinc

1 Preheat the oven to 200°C (400°F, gas mark 6). To make filling, put the red and yellow peppers and the courgettes in a roasting tin, drizzle over the oil and turn the vegetables to coat. Sprinkle over the garlic and thyme sprigs, and roast for 15 minutes.

2 Add the tomatoes to the tin and roast for a further 10 minutes. Season the vegetables with salt and pepper to taste, and set aside.

3 Roll out the pastry dough thinly on a lightly floured surface to make a rectangle about 30 x 40 cm (12 x 16 in). Use the pastry to line an 18 x 25 cm (7 x 10 in) non-stick baking tin that is 3 cm (1¼ in) deep. Reserve the pastry trimmings.

4 Prick the bottom of the pastry case. Bake it 'blind' (see page 19) for 10 minutes, then remove the paper and beans, and bake for a further 5 minutes or until golden.

5 Fill the pastry case with the roasted vegetables, spreading them out evenly. Scatter over the feta cheese.

6 Roll out the pastry trimmings and cut into thin strips. Lay the strips in a criss-cross pattern over the filling to make a lattice. Brush the pastry strips with the milk and sprinkle them with the poppy seeds, if using.

7 Bake for 15–20 minutes or until the pastry lattice is golden brown. Serve the tart hot or cold, cut across into thin slices or squares.

Plus points

• Olive oil pastry is lower in saturated fat than shortcrust made with butter. Most of the fatty acids in olive oil are monounsaturated, which are thought to play a part in lowering high blood cholesterol levels.

• Feta cheese has a medium fat content. It is salty, so if you are watching your sodium intake soak the cheese in milk for 15–20 minutes before use (discard the milk).

• Peppers are an excellent source of vitamin C and beta-carotene. Their beta-carotene content depends on the colour of the pepper, with red peppers having the most and green peppers the least.

Some more ideas

• Instead of feta, use Caerphilly or Lancashire cheese.

• Make a Puy lentil and goat's cheese slice. For the filling, soften 1 chopped onion in 1 tbsp extra virgin olive oil with 1 crushed garlic clove and 2 tsp finely chopped, fresh root ginger. Add 200 g (7 oz) Puy lentils, 1 can of chopped tomatoes, about 400 g, with the juice, and 250 ml (8½ fl oz) vegetable stock. Bring to the boil, then reduce the heat and simmer for 10 minutes. Add 250 g (8½ oz) peeled and diced potatoes and cook for 10 minutes, then add 125 g (4½ oz) frozen peas. Bring back to the boil and cook for a further 5–10 minutes or until the potatoes and lentils are tender. Add a little more stock if needed. Stir in 50 g (1¾ oz) chopped watercress and season to taste. Spread evenly in the pastry case and scatter over 100 g (3½ oz) crumbled goat's cheese. Make a lattice top with the pastry trimmings, twisting the strips. Brush with milk and sprinkle with 1–2 tsp fennel seeds, if liked. Bake as in the main recipe.

Venison and mushroom pie

A sweet potato mash flavoured with mustard and orange is the colourful top for this winter pie. Underneath is a hearty and rich-tasting filling of lean venison simmered in red wine with baby onions and button mushrooms. Some simple green vegetables are all that's needed to balance this delicious dish.

Serves 4

2 tbsp extra virgin olive oil

200 g (7 oz) small button onions, peeled and left whole

500 g (1 lb 2 oz) boneless haunch of venison or venison shoulder, diced

150 g (5½ oz) baby button mushrooms

3 celery sticks, thickly sliced

1 tbsp fresh thyme leaves

300 ml (10 fl oz) full-bodied red wine

150 ml (5 fl oz) strong beef stock

1½ tbsp cornflour

salt and pepper

Sweet potato mash

1 kg (2¼ lb) sweet potatoes, cubed

1 tbsp wholegrain mustard

grated zest and juice of 1 orange

Preparation time: 1¼ hours

Cooking time: 20 minutes

Each serving provides

kcal 500, **protein** 33 g, **fat** 9 g (of which saturated fat 2 g), **carbohydrate** 64 g (of which sugars 19 g), **fibre** 8 g

✓✓✓	A, C, E, copper, zinc
✓✓	B₁, iron, potassium, selenium
✓	B₂, B₆, folate, niacin, calcium

1 Heat the oil in a large saucepan and add the onions. Cover and cook over a low heat for 8–10 minutes, shaking the pan occasionally, until the onions are lightly browned all over.

2 Remove the onions to a plate using a draining spoon. Add the venison to the pan and cook, uncovered, over a moderately high heat for 2–3 minutes or until the cubes are well browned.

3 Add the onions, mushrooms, celery and thyme. Pour in the wine and stock. Bring to the boil, then reduce the heat. Cover and simmer for 45 minutes or until the venison is tender.

4 Meanwhile, steam the sweet potatoes for 25 minutes or until tender. Alternatively, cook them in boiling water for 15 minutes, then drain.

5 Preheat the oven to 190°C (375°F, gas mark 5). Tip the sweet potatoes into a bowl and mash with the mustard, orange zest and juice, and salt and pepper to taste. Set aside.

6 Blend the cornflour with 2 tbsp cold water. Stir into the venison mixture and cook, stirring, until lightly thickened. Season to taste. Spoon the filling into a 1.2 litre (2 pint) pie dish.

7 Spread the sweet potato mash over the venison filling to cover it completely. Bake for 20 minutes. Serve the pie hot.

Some more ideas

• The pie can be made ahead and chilled, then reheated in a preheated 190°C (375°F, gas mark 5) oven for 45 minutes or until piping hot.

• Cover the venison filling with a potato and butternut mash. Steam 500 g (1 lb 2 oz) each peeled potatoes and butternut squash for 25 minutes, or cook in boiling water for about 15 minutes, until tender. Mash with 15 g (½ oz) butter and 2 tbsp snipped fresh chives.

• For a rabbit pie, lightly brown 400 g (14 oz) boneless diced rabbit in 1 tbsp extra virgin olive oil with 100 g (3½ oz) diced smoked bacon. Add 2 large sliced leeks, 3 sliced carrots and 2 parsnips, cut into chunks. Stir in 300 ml (10 fl oz) white wine, 150 ml (5 fl oz) chicken stock and 1 tbsp Dijon mustard. Simmer, covered, for 45 minutes. Cover with the sweet potato mash, or the potato and butternut mash, and bake as in the main recipe.

Plus points

• Venison is a particularly low-fat meat, containing even less fat than chicken. It is a rich source of B vitamins and contains twice as much iron as beef.

• Sweet potatoes are an excellent source of beta-carotene. They contain more vitamin E than any other vegetable and are a good source of vitamin C.

Chillied potato and leek quiche

If you love quiche but are tired of the usual fillings, here's a new idea to whet your appetite. A vibrant green layer of peppery rocket is sandwiched between sliced potatoes and leeks in a Gruyère-flavoured custard, and the crisp pastry case is speckled with hot chilli and fragrant thyme. Serve warm with a tomato and red onion salad.

Serves 4

Sunflower oil shortcrust pastry

170 g (6 oz) plain flour

2 fresh red chillies, seeded and finely chopped

2 tsp chopped fresh thyme

1 egg

4 tbsp sunflower oil

1 tbsp tepid water

Potato and leek filling

350 g (12½ oz) waxy new potatoes, scrubbed

250 g (8½ oz) leeks, cut into 1 cm (½ in) slices

55 g (2 oz) Gruyère cheese, grated

2 tbsp snipped fresh chives

55 g (2 oz) rocket, roughly chopped

2 eggs

150 ml (5 fl oz) semi-skimmed milk

salt and pepper

Preparation time: 30 minutes, plus 30 minutes resting

Cooking time: 40–45 minutes

Each serving provides Ⓥ

kcal 459, **protein** 17 g, **fat** 22 g (of which saturated fat 6 g), **carbohydrate** 51 g (of which sugars 5 g), **fibre** 4 g

✓✓✓	B$_{12}$, E
✓✓	A, B$_1$, B$_6$, C, folate, calcium
✓	B$_2$, niacin, iron, copper, potassium, selenium, zinc

---

1 To make the pastry, sift the flour and a pinch of salt into a bowl. Stir in the chillies and thyme, then make a well in the centre. Whisk together the egg, oil and water, add to the dry ingredients and quickly mix together with a fork to make a dough.

2 Turn out the dough onto a lightly floured surface and knead for a few seconds until smooth. Put into a bowl, cover with a damp tea-towel and leave to rest for about 30 minutes before rolling out.

3 Meanwhile, make the filling. Cook the potatoes in boiling water for 10–12 minutes or until almost tender. Steam the leeks over the potatoes for 6–7 minutes, or cook them in a separate pan of boiling water for 4–5 minutes, until tender. Drain thoroughly and leave until cool enough to handle.

4 Preheat the oven to 200°C (400°F, gas mark 6) and put a baking sheet in to heat. Roll out the pastry dough thinly and use to line a 20 cm (8 in) round, loose-bottomed, fluted flan tin about 3 cm (1¼ in) deep. Scatter half the cheese over the bottom of the case.

5 Thickly slice the warm potatoes and toss with the leeks, the remaining cheese, the chives, and salt and pepper to taste. Arrange half of the potato and leek mixture in a layer in the pastry

case. Scatter over the chopped rocket, then spread the rest of the potato and leek mixture on top.

6 Lightly beat the eggs together in a jug. Heat the milk to just below boiling point, then add to the eggs, whisking gently to mix.

7 Place the tin on the hot baking sheet and carefully pour the warm egg custard into the pastry case. Bake for 10 minutes, then reduce the oven temperature to 180°C (350°F, gas mark 4). Bake for a further 30–35 minutes or until the filling is lightly set. Leave in the tin for 5 minutes before removing. Serve warm.

Plus points

• Chillies contain more vitamin C, weight for weight, than citrus fruit. But the quantity of chillies usually eaten means the overall intake of this vitamin is not huge.

• Rocket, like other dark green leafy vegetables, is a good source of folate, a vitamin involved in the production of red blood cells.

• Like many other cheeses, Gruyère is high in saturated fat, which makes it a good source of fat-soluble vitamins such as A and D.

Some more ideas

• For a higher fibre pastry, use half white flour and half wholemeal flour. You'll need an extra 2 tsp water to mix the dough together.

• To make a sweet potato and Swiss chard quiche, cut 350 g (12½ oz) sweet potatoes into cubes slightly larger than 1 cm (½ in) and cook in boiling water for 4 minutes or until almost tender. Shred 170 g (6 oz) Swiss chard (or baby leaf greens) and steam for 4 minutes, or cook in a separate pan of boiling water for about 4 minutes, until tender but still crisp. Drain thoroughly, squeezing out excess moisture. Toss the sweet potatoes with the chard or greens, 25 g (scant 1 oz) coarsely grated Emmenthal cheese, and seasoning to taste. Scatter a further 30 g (1 oz) grated Emmenthal over the bottom of the pastry case. Pack the vegetable mixture into the pastry case, levelling the surface, and pour over the egg custard. Bake as in the main recipe and serve warm.

Pork, prune and orange pie

Hot water crust, traditionally used for raised pies, makes a tasty lid for this pie, showing how classic pastries can be used in new and different ways. It covers a savoury filling of pork and prunes cooked in apple juice with orange zest and sage. Serve with boiled potatoes and seasonal green vegetables.

Serves 4

1 quantity Hot-water crust pastry (see page 24)

Pork and prune filling

1 tbsp sunflower oil

400 g (14 oz) pork fillet (tenderloin), trimmed of all fat and cut into bite-sized pieces

2 leeks, sliced

150 ml (5 fl oz) apple juice

200 ml (7 fl oz) pork, chicken or vegetable stock

1 tbsp dry sherry

grated zest of 1 orange

1 tbsp chopped fresh sage or 1 tsp dried sage

170 g (6 oz) ready-to-eat stoned prunes

2 tsp cornflour

salt and pepper

Preparation time: 50 minutes (including making the pastry)

Cooking time: 35 minutes

Each serving provides

kcal 422, **protein** 27 g, **fat** 15 g (of which saturated fat 4 g), **carbohydrate** 46 g (of which sugars 21 g), **fibre** 5 g

✓ A, B$_1$, B$_6$, C, E, folate, calcium, copper, iron, potassium

1 To make the filling, heat the oil in a large non-stick frying pan over a moderately high heat. Add the pieces of pork and cook for 3–4 minutes or until lightly browned on all sides. Remove to a plate using a draining spoon. Add the leeks to the frying pan and cook for 2–3 minutes or until softened.

2 Add the apple juice, stock, sherry, orange zest and sage. Bring to the boil, then reduce the heat. Return the pork to the pan and add the prunes. Cover and cook gently for 20 minutes or until the pork is tender. Preheat the oven to 220°C (425°F, gas mark 7).

3 Using a draining spoon, transfer the pork, prunes and vegetables to a 1.2 litre (2 pint) pie dish. Blend the cornflour with 2 tsp cold water, then stir into the cooking liquid left in the pan. Bring to the boil, stirring, and cook until the sauce has thickened slightly. Season with salt and pepper to taste, then pour into the pie dish.

4 Roll out the pastry dough thinly to a round or oval to cover the pie dish. Lay the dough over the filling, crimp the edges and make a small hole in the centre so the steam can escape.

5 Bake for 15 minutes, then reduce the oven temperature to 180°C (350°F, gas mark 4). Bake for a further 20 minutes or until golden. Serve hot.

Some more ideas

• Use skinless, boneless chicken breasts (fillets) instead of pork, and ready-to-eat dried apricots rather than prunes.

• Make a duck pie with port and cranberries. Skin 4 duck breasts and cut into bite-sized pieces, then sear in 1 tbsp sunflower oil in a non-stick pan for 3–4 minutes. Remove the duck to a plate. Add 1 chopped onion to the pan and cook for 5 minutes or until softened. Stir in 300 ml (10 fl oz) chicken stock, 2 tbsp port, 1 tbsp cranberry sauce and a piece of chopped stem ginger, drained of syrup. Bring to the boil, then reduce the heat. Return the duck to the pan and add 2–3 sliced carrots. Cover and simmer gently for 20 minutes. Add 85 g (3 oz) fresh or frozen cranberries for the last 5 minutes of the cooking time. Spoon the filling into the pie dish using a draining spoon. Thicken the liquid with cornflour as in the main recipe and season to taste. Pour into the pie dish, top with the hot-water crust and bake as in the main recipe.

Plus points

• Pork is much lower in fat than it was 20 years ago because of the breeding methods used by farmers today.

• Prunes are a good source of dietary fibre and contain a natural laxative.

savoury dishes for entertaining

94

Pesto rice pie with mozzarella

This open pie, with its richly flavoured 'risotto' crust and Mediterranean vegetable filling topped with melting cubes of soft mozzarella, looks wonderful and tastes sensational! Serve with a chunky green salad of chopped celery and chicory tossed with a little plain low-fat yogurt and chopped fresh mint.

Serves 4

Risotto crust

15 g (½ oz) butter

1 small onion, finely chopped

200 g (7 oz) risotto rice

600 ml (1 pint) hot vegetable stock

1 garlic clove, roughly chopped

25 g (scant 1 oz) fresh basil

25 g (scant 1 oz) Parmesan cheese, freshly grated

15 g (½ oz) pine nuts

1 tbsp extra virgin olive oil

finely grated zest of 1 lemon

1 small egg, beaten

salt and pepper

Mozzarella filling

1 tbsp extra virgin olive oil

1 red onion, sliced

300 g (10½ oz) courgettes, thickly sliced

250 g (8½ oz) tomatoes, cut into chunks

125 g (4½ oz) mozzarella cheese, diced

fresh basil leaves to garnish

Preparation and cooking time: 1¼ hours

Each serving provides Ⓥ

kcal 467, **protein** 19 g, **fat** 23 g (of which saturated fat 9 g), **carbohydrate** 45 g (of which sugars 6 g), **fibre** 2 g

---

✓✓✓ A

✓✓ B₁₂, C, niacin, calcium, copper, zinc

✓ B₁, B₂, B₆, E, folate, iron, potassium

---

1 Preheat the oven to 190°C (375°F, gas mark 5). First make the risotto for the crust. Melt the butter in a large, wide pan and cook the onion gently for 4–5 minutes, stirring, until just softened but not browned. Add the rice and stir for 1 minute.

2 Add a ladleful of the hot stock and bubble over a moderate heat, stirring, until it is almost all absorbed, then add another ladleful of stock. Continue adding the stock gradually in this way, stirring frequently. When all the stock has been added and absorbed, the rice should be just tender and the risotto creamy. Remove from the heat.

3 Place the garlic, basil, Parmesan cheese, pine nuts and olive oil in a blender or food processor, and blend together until finely chopped. Stir into the rice with the lemon zest, egg, and salt and pepper to taste.

4 Spoon the risotto mixture into a straight-sided 23 cm (9 in) loose-bottomed flan tin about 3 cm (1¼ in) deep. Spread evenly over the bottom and sides. Set the tin on a baking sheet and bake for 20 minutes or until the crust is lightly browned and just firm.

5 Meanwhile, for the filling, heat the oil in a large pan and cook the onion and courgettes for 3 minutes, stirring, until lightly coloured. Stir in the tomatoes, cover and cook over a moderate heat, shaking the pan occasionally, for 8–10 minutes or until the courgettes are just tender.

6 Spoon the vegetables into the risotto case and level the surface. Scatter the mozzarella over the top. Bake for 8–10 minutes or until the cheese is melted and bubbling. Serve hot, garnished with basil leaves.

Plus points

• Apart from the nutritional benefits of rice, it has been used in natural medicine to treat a variety of digestive problems including indigestion, mild diarrhoea and constipation.

• Pesto, a classic Italian sauce, has a high fat content because of the inclusion of olive oil, pine nuts and Parmesan cheese. However, the majority of fat is present as the more healthy monounsaturated fat rather than saturated fat.

• Mozzarella cheese is lower in fat than many other cheeses and as a result is also lower in calories.

Some more ideas

• To save time, replace the basil, Parmesan cheese, pine nut and olive oil mixture with about 4 tbsp pesto sauce from a jar.

• For an aubergine and halloumi rice pie, make the risotto as in the main recipe up to the end of step 2, adding a pinch of saffron threads to the stock. Instead of the pesto mixture, flavour with 25 g (scant 1 oz) toasted chopped almonds, 2 tbsp chopped fresh mint and the finely grated zest of 1 orange. Stir in the beaten egg and seasoning to taste, then finish the risotto case as in the main recipe. For the filling, fry 3 crushed garlic cloves in 2 tbsp extra virgin olive oil for 30 seconds. Add 375 g (13 oz) diced aubergine and cook on a high heat, stirring, for 10 minutes or until softened and lightly browned. Add 1 can of chopped tomatoes, about 400 g, with the juice, and simmer for 5 minutes or until most of the juice has evaporated. Spoon into the risotto case, top with 125 g (4½ oz) diced halloumi cheese and bake for 8–10 minutes or until golden. Serve hot, garnished with sprigs of fresh mint.

Guinea fowl pudding

Guinea fowl cooked with shallots, 'meaty' chestnut mushrooms, peas and spinach in Madeira wine makes a great pie filling. In this modern version of a traditional favourite, the filling is baked in a pudding basin topped with a lovely, soft-textured potato pastry crust. Serve with Brussels sprouts and baby carrots.

Serves 4

1 quantity Herbed potato pastry (see Some more ideas, page 24) with 1 tbsp chopped fresh tarragon added, chilled for 30 minutes

Guinea fowl filling

2 tbsp extra virgin olive oil

250 g (8½ oz) small shallots, peeled and left whole

400 g (14 oz) skinless boneless guinea fowl breasts (fillets), cubed

250 g (8½ oz) chestnut mushrooms, halved

2 garlic cloves, crushed

90 ml (3 fl oz) Madeira

150 ml (5 fl oz) well-flavoured chicken stock

2 tbsp cornflour

85 g (3 oz) frozen petit pois

100 g (3½ oz) baby spinach leaves

1 tbsp chopped fresh tarragon

salt and pepper

Preparation time: 55 minutes (including making the pastry), plus 30 minutes chilling

Cooking time: 40 minutes

Each serving provides

kcal 536, **protein** 30 g, **fat** 23 g (of which saturated fat 10 g), **carbohydrate** 50 g (of which sugars 6 g), **fibre** 5 g

✓✓✓	A, B₆, niacin, copper
✓✓	B₁, C, folate, potassium, selenium, zinc
✓	B₂, E, calcium, iron

1 Place the potato pastry dough on a large piece of cling film on the work surface. Press out the dough with your hands to make a round that is slightly larger than the top of a 1.4 litre (2½ pint) pudding basin. Lay another sheet of cling film on top and roll up the dough round. Chill while making the filling.

2 Heat the oil in a large saucepan and add the shallots. Cover and cook gently for 8–10 minutes, shaking the pan occasionally, until the shallots are lightly browned all over.

3 Add the guinea fowl to the pan, increase the heat to moderate and cook, uncovered, for 3–4 minutes or until the cubes are no longer pink on the outside, stirring so they cook evenly.

4 Add the mushrooms and garlic. Pour in the Madeira and stock, and bring to the boil. Reduce the heat, cover and cook gently for 10 minutes. Preheat the oven to 190°C (375°F, gas mark 5).

5 Blend the cornflour with 2 tbsp cold water to make a paste. Add to the pan and cook gently, stirring, until the liquid has thickened. Add the petit pois, spinach and tarragon, and season with salt and pepper to taste. Stir for a few more seconds or until the spinach has wilted. Spoon the mixture into the pudding basin.

6 Unwrap the potato pastry round and place it over the top of the pudding basin. Press the edges onto the rim of the basin, pinching them well to seal. Make a hole in the middle so that steam can escape.

7 Set the basin on a baking sheet and bake for 40 minutes or until the pastry is golden brown and the filling is bubbling. Serve immediately.

Plus points

• Originally a game bird, guinea fowl is now classified as poultry. Like chicken it is another low-fat source of protein, especially if the skin is removed, as in this recipe, and it provides B vitamins and iron.

• When potatoes were first introduced into Europe they were believed to have 'weakening' properties. More recently they have been considered fattening. In fact potatoes are very nutritious and low in fat, which makes them a useful food to include in a healthy diet.

• Shallots, a variety of onion, tend to have a much milder and subtler flavour than the onion itself. Like the onion, they contain some vitamin C and B vitamins.

Some more ideas

• Instead of guinea fowl, you can use chicken or turkey breast fillets, as well as skinless boneless pheasant or duck breasts.

• The pastry dough and filling can be prepared ahead of time, then the pie assembled and baked just before serving.

• This is a good way to use up leftover cooked poultry. Skip step 3, and add the diced skinless, boneless poultry with the spinach. Heat through, then spoon into the pudding basin, cover with the pastry lid and bake as in the main recipe.

• For a Chinese chicken and corn pudding, stir-fry 400 g (14 oz) diced skinless, boneless chicken breasts (fillets) in 2 tbsp groundnut oil with 2 crushed garlic cloves for 3–4 minutes. Add 1 seeded and chopped fresh red chilli, 1 tbsp finely chopped, fresh root ginger, 250 g (8½ oz) halved chestnut mushrooms and 150 g (5½ oz) baby corn, sliced at an angle. Stir-fry for 1–2 minutes, then stir in 90 ml (3 fl oz) each dry sherry and water, 2 tbsp light soy sauce, 1 tbsp clear honey and ½ tsp 5-spice powder. Simmer for 10 minutes, covered, then thicken with cornflour as in the main recipe. Add 100 g (3½ oz) shredded spring greens and 4 chopped spring onions. Pile into the pudding basin and top with the potato pastry crust (flavoured with 1 tbsp chopped fresh coriander instead of tarragon). Bake as in the main recipe.

Prawn and couscous filo crown

Here is an impressive filo pastry dish for entertaining. The filling is made with couscous, coloured golden with saffron, prawns, tomatoes, peas, spring onions and coriander. Rocket leaves add a contrasting, fresh green layer through the centre. Serve hot or cold for a special meal for 6, or as the centrepiece of a buffet for 8.

Serves 6

7 sheets filo pastry, 30 x 50 cm (12 x 20 in) each, about 210 g (7¼ oz) in total

2 tbsp extra virgin olive oil

1 tbsp sesame seeds

Couscous filling

300 g (10½ oz) couscous

large pinch of saffron threads

1 tsp harissa or chilli paste

500 ml (17 fl oz) boiling vegetable stock

100 g (3½ oz) frozen peas

250 g (8½ oz) cooked, peeled tiger prawns

200 g (7 oz) tomatoes, skinned, seeded and chopped

3 spring onions, finely chopped

20 g (¾ oz) fresh coriander, chopped

grated zest and juice of 1 lemon

50 g (1¾ oz) rocket leaves

salt and pepper

Preparation time: 40–45 minutes

Cooking time: 20 minutes

Each serving provides

kcal 318, **protein** 18 g, **fat** 7 g (of which saturated fat 1 g), **carbohydrate** 49 g (of which sugars 2 g), **fibre** 2 g

✓✓✓ B_{12}

✓ B_1, C, niacin, calcium, copper, iron, selenium, zinc

1 First make the filling. Put the couscous in a bowl. Add the saffron and harissa to the boiling stock and pour over the couscous. Stir and leave to soak for 10 minutes. All the stock should be absorbed.

2 Meanwhile, cook the peas in a pan of boiling water for 4–5 minutes, or according to the packet instructions. Drain. Preheat the oven to 190°C (375°F, gas mark 5).

3 Rub the couscous between your fingers to separate the grains. Add the peas, prawns, tomatoes, spring onions, coriander, and lemon zest and juice. Mix well and season to taste.

4 Lay a sheet of filo pastry out on the work surface with the short sides to the left and right. (Keep the rest of the filo covered to prevent it from drying out.) Brush very lightly with olive oil. Lay a second sheet of filo above the first so that the long edges overlap by about 10 cm (4 in). Brush this sheet very lightly with olive oil.

5 Lay a third sheet of filo to the right of the first 2 sheets, placing it so a long side overlaps the edges by about 12.5 cm (5 in), to make a rectangle about 67.5 x 50 cm (27 x 20 in). Brush lightly with oil. Repeat with 3 more filo sheets, laying them on top of the first so the rectangle is double thickness.

6 Arrange the rocket leaves in a line near a long side of the pastry rectangle. Pile the couscous mixture evenly on top. Brush the pastry edges with oil, then carefully roll up to make a long sausage shape. Carefully lift onto a non-stick baking sheet and curve round so that the ends meet, to make a circle. Seal the ends together. Brush the pastry ring very lightly all over with oil.

7 Cut the remaining sheet of filo into strips, scrunch them up and arrange on the top of the ring. Brush with the remaining oil and sprinkle with the sesame seeds. Bake for 20 minutes or until golden brown.

Plus points

• Couscous is a staple of many North African countries. Made from semolina, it provides an interesting starchy carbohydrate alternative to rice, pasta or potatoes.

• Filo pastry is lower in fat than many other pastries, especially puff and flaky, and always looks impressive for a special occasion.

• Both prawns and sesame seeds provide good amounts of calcium, essential for keeping bones healthy and strong.

savoury dishes for entertaining

Another idea

• Try a bulghur wheat and smoked trout strudel. Soak 300 g (10½ oz) bulghur wheat in 600 ml (1 pint) boiling vegetable stock, mixed with the harissa, for 30 minutes. Drain off any excess liquid, then stir in the tomatoes and lemon zest and juice (omit the peas, prawns and spring onions). Add 20 g (¾ oz) each chopped parsley and snipped fresh chives, and fold in 200 g (7 oz) flaked smoked trout fillet. Instead of rocket, arrange 85 g (3 oz) roughly chopped watercress on the filo rectangle. Spoon the bulghur wheat filling on top. Fold in the short sides, then roll up to make a sausage shape. Lay diagonally on a baking sheet, without curving into a circle, and top with the scrunched filo. Brush with oil, sprinkle with sesame seeds and bake as in the main recipe.

Deluxe asparagus tart

The filling for this very special tart combines asparagus spears with strips of Parma ham, peas and grated pecorino cheese in a garlic-flavoured egg custard. The pastry case is made from a light yeasted shortcrust that is surprisingly low in fat. Small minted new potatoes would make a perfect accompaniment.

Serves 4

Yeasted pastry

140 g (5 oz) plain flour

45 g (1½ oz) cool butter, diced

1 tsp easy-blend dried yeast

1 egg

2 tbsp tepid water

Garlicky asparagus filling

4 garlic cloves, unpeeled

250 g (8½ oz) slender asparagus spears, cut across in half

30 g (1 oz) pecorino cheese, finely grated

50 g (1¾ oz) Parma ham, trimmed of fat and cut into thin strips

50 g (1¾ oz) frozen peas, thawed

2 eggs

1 egg yolk

250 ml (8½ fl oz) semi-skimmed milk

salt and pepper

Preparation time: 30 minutes, plus 45 minutes resting

Cooking time: 30–35 minutes

Each serving provides

kcal 400, **protein** 21 g, **fat** 21 g (of which saturated fat 11 g), **carbohydrate** 33 g (of which sugars 5 g), **fibre** 3 g

✓✓✓	B₁₂
✓✓	A, folate, calcium, zinc
✓	B₁, B₂, B₆, C, E, niacin, copper, iron, potassium, selenium

1 To make the pastry, sift the flour and a pinch of salt into a bowl, and rub in the butter until the mixture resembles fine breadcrumbs. Stir in the yeast. Lightly beat the egg with the water, and sprinkle over the rubbed-in mixture. Gather together to make a dough.

2 Turn out the pastry dough onto a lightly floured surface and knead briefly until smooth. Put it back into the bowl, cover with cling film and set aside to rest at room temperature for about 45 minutes.

3 Meanwhile, prepare the filling. Put the garlic cloves in the bottom of a steamer with about 5 cm (2 in) of hot water. Place the stalk halves of the asparagus spears in the top of the steamer and steam for 1 minute on a moderate heat. Add the asparagus tips and steam for a further 1–1½ minutes or until just beginning to soften. (Thicker spears may need a few minutes longer.) Remove the asparagus and garlic, and set aside.

4 Preheat the oven to 200°C (400°F, gas mark 6) and put a baking sheet in to heat. Roll out the pastry dough thinly (there's no need to knead it again) on a lightly floured surface and use to line a 25 cm (10 in) loose-bottomed, shallow flan tin.

5 Scatter the pecorino cheese over the bottom of the pastry case, then arrange the asparagus and Parma ham on top, filling the gaps with peas.

6 Squeeze the softened garlic from the skins and mash to a paste. Whisk in the eggs, egg yolk, and salt and pepper to taste. Heat the milk to boiling point, then pour over the egg mixture, whisking to mix.

7 Place the flan tin on the hot baking sheet. Pour the egg custard into the tart. Bake for 5 minutes, then reduce the oven temperature to 180°C (350°F, gas mark 4). Bake for a further 25–30 minutes or until the filling is lightly set and the pastry is golden brown.

8 Leave the tart to stand for about 5 minutes before removing it from the tin. Serve hot or warm, cut into wedges.

Plus points

• Asparagus contains the phytochemical asparagine, which has diuretic properties. Indeed, the ancient Greeks used asparagus in the treatment of kidney problems.

• Parma ham makes a good lean alternative to bacon, especially if any visible fat is trimmed away, as in this recipe.

savoury dishes for entertaining

Some more ideas

• Use freshly grated Parmesan cheese in place of the pecorino.

• For a courgette and blue cheese tart, steam 400 g (14 oz) courgettes, cut into 1 cm (½ in) slices, for 3 minutes, adding the garlic cloves to the water as in the main recipe. Remove the courgettes and pat dry with kitchen paper. Arrange them in the pastry case and scatter over 50 g (1¾ oz) crumbled blue cheese such as Stilton or Roquefort and 30 g (1 oz) roughly chopped walnuts. Make the garlic custard using 3 whole eggs, 200 ml (7 fl oz) semi-skimmed milk, and salt and pepper to taste. Bake as in the main recipe.

Sweet Pies and Tarts

Tempting pastries for all occasions

Pastry and crushed biscuits provide the cases and bases for this delectable assortment of sweet treats. Shortcrust enriched with almonds makes little tartlets filled with luscious berries under a featherlight meringue, while spiced shortcrust wrapped freeform round apples and blueberries is the easiest fruit pie you could wish for. Use filo for a simple strudel filled with fresh cherries, or to make a very pretty lattice topping on a redcurrant tart. Crushed amaretti are the base for a baked cheesecake adorned with fruit – an impressive finale for any meal.

Kiwi-berry cheesecake tart

Impress your family and friends with this tempting baked cheesecake tart, piled high with vitamin C-rich strawberries and kiwi fruit. Unlike many cheesecakes that are high in fat and calories, this recipe uses a lower fat soft cheese for the filling and a crushed amaretti biscuit base made without butter.

Serves 10

115 g (4 oz) amaretti biscuits, crushed

450 g (1 lb) curd cheese

3 eggs, separated

115 g (4 oz) caster sugar

finely grated zest of 1 small orange

150 ml (5 fl oz) whipping cream

30 g (1 oz) plain flour

Fruit topping

300 g (10½ oz) strawberries, halved or sliced

2 kiwi fruit, peeled and sliced

1 tbsp icing sugar, sifted

Preparation time: 30 minutes

Cooking time: 1¼ hours

1 Preheat the oven to 160°C (325°F, gas mark 3). Grease a 20 cm (8 in) springform tin and line the bottom with greaseproof paper. Sprinkle the amaretti biscuit crumbs evenly over the paper lining on the bottom and set aside.

2 Put the curd cheese, egg yolks, caster sugar, orange zest and cream in a blender or food processor. Blend until smooth and well mixed, then pour the mixture into a bowl. (Alternatively, beat the ingredients together with an electric mixer.) Sift the flour over the surface and fold it in.

3 In a separate clean, grease-free bowl, whisk the egg whites until stiff. Gently fold them into the cheese mixture. Pour into the tin, without disturbing the biscuit crumbs, and level the surface.

4 Bake for 1¼ hours or until slightly risen, lightly set and golden brown. Turn off the oven and leave the tart inside for 15 minutes, then remove and set aside to cool completely. If you like, chill before serving.

5 Remove the cheesecake tart from the tin and place it on a serving plate. Pile the strawberries and kiwi over the top and dust with the icing sugar. Cut into slices to serve.

Some more ideas

• Use the finely grated zest of 1 small pink grapefruit or 1 lime in place of the orange zest.

• Instead of amaretti, sprinkle 140 g (5 oz) crushed digestive or oaty biscuits over the bottom of the tin.

• Top the cheesecake tart with a mixture of sliced peaches or nectarines and blueberries.

• For a raspberry cheesecake tart, sprinkle 140 g (5 oz) crushed ginger biscuits over the bottom of the cake tin. Make the cheesecake mixture as in the main recipe, but using ricotta cheese in place of curd cheese, light soft brown sugar in place of caster sugar and the finely grated zest of 1 lemon in place of the orange zest. After baking, decorate the top with 350 g (12½ oz) fresh raspberries and dust with sifted icing sugar.

Plus points

• Curd cheese contains about half the amount of fat that is found in hard cheeses such as Cheddar.

• Kiwi fruits are an excellent source of vitamin C – a single fruit supplies enough to meet the daily requirement for this vitamin.

Each serving provides Ⓥ

kcal 287, **protein** 8 g, **fat** 15 g (of which saturated fat 8 g), **carbohydrate** 31 g (of which sugars 19 g), **fibre** 1 g

✓✓	A, C
✓	B$_{12}$

Brandied mincemeat purses

Here are some luxurious little 'moneybag' pastries filled with a ginger-spiced mixture of dried fruit, apple and walnuts. The dried fruits are first soaked in brandy, although you can replace the alcohol with fresh orange juice if you prefer. Try these at Christmas-time as a lower-fat alternative to mince pies.

Serves 6 (makes 12 pastries)

6 sheets filo pastry, 30 x 50 cm (12 x 20 in) each, about 180 g (6¼ oz) in total

45 g (1½ oz) unsalted butter, melted

1 tbsp icing sugar, sifted

Mincemeat filling

150 g (5½ oz) mixed dried fruit, such as sultanas, raisins, currants and diced peel

4 tbsp brandy

1 cooking apple, about 250 g (8½ oz)

30 g (1 oz) preserved stem ginger, finely chopped

25 g (scant 1 oz) chopped walnuts

finely grated zest of 1 small lemon

Preparation time: about 25 minutes, plus 1 hour soaking

Cooking time: 12–15 minutes

1 To make the filling, place the dried fruit in a bowl with the brandy and stir. Cover and leave to soak for 1 hour or until the brandy has been absorbed.

2 Preheat the oven to 200°C (400°F, gas mark 6). Peel, core and coarsely grate the apple. Add to the soaked dried fruit together with the ginger, walnuts and lemon zest. Mix well together.

3 Lay the sheets of filo out, stacking them on top of each other. Cut the stack into six 15 cm (6 in) squares, trimming off the excess pastry. You will have 36 squares. Brush each square very lightly with melted butter and layer them, with the corners offset, to make 12 stacks of 3 squares each.

4 Place about 1 tbsp of the fruit mixture on each stack, then gather up the edges and pinch together at the top to enclose the filling.

5 Place the pastries on a non-stick baking sheet and brush lightly with the remaining butter. Bake for 12–15 minutes or until golden brown. Serve warm, dusted with icing sugar.

Some more ideas

• For an unusual scented flavour, replace the brandy with cold Earl Grey tea, or with a fruit tea such as apple and ginger.

• To make date and apricot parcels, place 115 g (4 oz) ready-to-eat dried apricots and

115 g (4 oz) stoned dates, both finely chopped, in a bowl with 4 tbsp orange juice. Stir, then leave to soak for 1 hour. Add the finely grated zest of ½ orange, 25 g (scant 1 oz) chopped pistachio nuts, ½ tsp ground cinnamon and ¼ tsp orange flower water. Cut 2 stacked sheets of filo pastry into 3 long strips, then cut each strip across in half to measure about 10 x 25 cm (4 x 10 in). Melt 20 g (¾ oz) butter and brush lightly over the 12 pastry strips. Place a rounded tbsp of the filling at one end of each strip. Fold one corner over the filling to make a triangular shape, then keep folding over down the length of the strip to make a triangular pastry. Brush lightly with the remaining butter, place on a baking sheet and bake for 12–15 minutes or until golden brown.

Each serving provides Ⓥ

kcal 314, **protein** 4.5 g, **fat** 10 g (of which saturated fat 4 g), **carbohydrate** 49 g (of which sugars 30 g), **fibre** 1 g

✓   A, C, copper

Plus points

• Dried fruit is naturally sweet with fructose, so no sugar is needed in this filling. Dried fruit is also a source of nutrients including dietary fibre, iron, calcium, phosphorus and some B vitamins.

• Herbalists use ginger for its anti-sickness properties and as an aid to digestion. It is also thought to protect against infections of the digestive and respiratory systems.

Meringue-topped berry tartlets

Make these irresistible tartlets at the height of summer when red berries and currants are in season. The luscious fruits fill tartlet cases made with a light almond pastry and are topped with crisp meringue.

Serves 6

1 quantity Sweet almond shortcrust pastry
(see Some more ideas, page 22),
chilled for 30 minutes

Fruit filling

200 g (7 oz) redcurrants

200 g (7 oz) blackcurrants

2 tbsp caster sugar

125 g (4½ oz) strawberries, chopped

1 tbsp redcurrant jelly

Meringue topping

2 egg whites

55 g (2 oz) caster sugar

Preparation and cooking time: about 1 hour
(including making the pastry), plus at
least 30 minutes chilling

Each serving provides Ⓥ

kcal 262, **protein** 5 g, **fat** 11 g (of which
saturated fat 6 g), **carbohydrate** 38 g (of
which sugars 27 g), **fibre** 3 g

✓✓✓	C
✓	A, E, calcium, copper, iron

1 Preheat the oven to 190°C (375°F, gas mark 5). To make the filling, put the red and blackcurrants in a saucepan with the caster sugar and cook very gently for 5 minutes or until the currants are softened but still holding their shape. Remove from the heat and stir in the strawberries and redcurrant jelly. Set aside.

2 Roll out the pastry dough thinly on a lightly floured work surface. Use to line 6 individual, loose-bottomed, non-stick tartlet tins 9 cm (3½ in) in diameter and 2.5 cm (1 in) deep.

3 Prick the tartlet cases and place on a baking sheet. Bake 'blind' (see page 19) for 10 minutes, then remove the paper and beans. Bake for a further 2–3 minutes or until light golden.

4 Remove the tartlet cases from the oven and set aside to cool. Reduce the oven temperature to 160°C (325°F, gas mark 3).

5 Meanwhile, make the meringue topping. Whisk the egg whites in a clean, grease-free bowl until stiff, then gradually whisk in the caster sugar to make a thick, glossy meringue.

6 Carefully remove the pastry cases from the tins and place back on the baking sheet. Fill with the fruit, using a draining spoon (discard any excess juice or use it elsewhere – see Some more ideas, right).

7 Top the tartlets with the meringue, swirling it gently to cover the fruit completely. Bake for 10–15 minutes or until the meringue is set and lightly golden. Serve warm or cold.

Plus points

• Egg whites do not contain any fat, but they are a source of protein and therefore can be a useful addition to a low-fat diet.

• Blackcurrants are an excellent source of vitamin C. On a weight for weight basis they contain 4 times as much vitamin C as oranges.

• Strawberries are not only an excellent source of vitamin C, they also contain the phytochemical ellagic acid, which is thought to help to protect against cancer.

Some more ideas

• When fresh currants and strawberries aren't available, use frozen fruits, thawing them and patting dry with kitchen paper. Or substitute other fruit such as raspberries or blueberries.

• Any juice drained from the fruit filling can be stirred into plain low-fat yogurt, added to a fruit salad or used in a milkshake or smoothie.

• Try gooseberry and apple meringue tartlets. Make the pastry with ground blanched hazelnuts instead of almonds. For the filling, gently cook 350 g (12½ oz) topped and tailed gooseberries and 1 peeled, cored and sliced cooking apple, about 300 g (10½ oz), with 30 g (1 oz) caster sugar for 10 minutes or until softened. Drain off any excess juice, then beat the fruit with a wooden spoon to make a rough purée (it doesn't need to be smooth). Taste and add a little extra sugar if needed. Divide the filling among the tartlet cases, top with meringue and bake as in the main recipe.

Cherry and almond strudel

Austria's famous melt-in-the-mouth pastry, here packed with juicy fresh cherries, looks very impressive, but is surprisingly easy to make. Ground almonds and breadcrumbs are added to the filling to absorb the fruit juices, so the layers of filo pastry bake wonderfully light and crisp.

Serves 6

3 sheets filo pastry, 30 x 50 cm (12 x 20 in) each, about 90 g (3¼ oz) in total

30 g (1 oz) butter, melted

15 g (½ oz) flaked almonds

1 tbsp icing sugar, sifted

Greek-style yogurt to serve (optional)

Cherry filling

30 g (1 oz) fresh white breadcrumbs

55 g (2 oz) ground almonds

45 g (1½ oz) soft light brown sugar

finely grated zest of 1 orange

675 g (1½ lb) fresh cherries, stoned and halved if large

Preparation time: 30–40 minutes

Cooking time: 20 minutes

1 Preheat the oven to 200°C (400°F, gas mark 6). To make the filling, stir the breadcrumbs, almonds, brown sugar and orange zest together in a large bowl. Add the cherries and mix well.

2 Lay a sheet of filo pastry out on a clean tea-towel and brush very lightly with melted butter. Place a second sheet of filo on top and brush very lightly with butter. Place the third sheet of filo on top and brush again with butter.

3 Spoon the filling evenly over the stacked pastry, leaving a 2.5 cm (1 in) margin clear around the edges. Turn in the edges of the short sides.

4 With the help of the tea-towel, roll up from a long side to make a thick sausage shape. Transfer to a lightly greased, non-stick baking tray, curving the strudel slightly to fit, if necessary. The seam should be underneath. Brush with the remaining butter, then scatter over the flaked almonds.

5 Bake for 20 minutes or until the pastry and almonds are golden brown. Dust with the icing sugar and serve hot or warm, with a little Greek-style yogurt, if liked.

Another idea

• For a plum, rum and raisin strudel, soak 50 g (1¾ oz) raisins in 2 tbsp dark rum for 1 hour. Mix with 675 g (1½ lb) sliced ripe plums, 75 g (2½ oz) fresh white breadcrumbs, 30 g (1 oz) chopped walnuts, 45 g (1½ oz) soft light brown sugar and the finely grated zest of 1 small lemon. Spread this filling over the filo pastry, roll up and bake as in the main recipe. Dust the hot strudel with 2 tsp icing sugar sifted with ½ tsp ground cinnamon.

Plus points

• Cherries are used all over the world in many famous dishes as well as being a key ingredient in liqueurs such as Kirsch and Maraschino. Like other fruits they are rich in potassium and they also contain a small amount of iron.

• Almonds are a good source of vitamin E, a powerful antioxidant that helps to protect against heart disease.

• Butter contains useful amounts of the fat-soluble vitamins A and D. Vitamin A is needed for healthy skin and vision. Vitamin D is required for the absorption of calcium and therefore has a vital role in maintaining strong teeth and bones.

Each serving provides

kcal 254, **protein** 5.5 g, **fat** 11 g (of which saturated fat 3 g), **carbohydrate** 36 g (of which sugars 24 g), **fibre** 2 g

✓✓	E
✓	C, copper

sweet pies and tarts

Topsy-turvy apple and sultana tart

This delectable tart is rather like the French tarte tatin, being turned out upside-down to serve. The pastry used is shortcrust made with reduced-fat soft cheese and butter, and there is a lot of juicy fruit filling.

Serves 4

Soft cheese shortcrust pastry

115 g (4 oz) plain flour

30 g (1 oz) cool unsalted butter, diced

30 g (1 oz) reduced-fat soft cheese

Apple and sultana filling

5 dessert apples, such as Cox's, about 600 g
    (1 lb 5 oz) in total

50 g (1¾ oz) light muscovado sugar

1 tbsp lemon juice

30 g (1 oz) sultanas

¼ tsp mixed spice

1 tsp finely grated lemon zest

Lemon and honey yogurt

250 g (8½ oz) plain low-fat yogurt

1 tbsp clear honey

1 tsp finely grated lemon zest

Preparation time: 45 minutes

Cooking time: 20 minutes

Each serving provides Ⓥ

kcal 345, **protein** 7.5 g, **fat** 8 g (of which saturated fat 5 g), **carbohydrate** 65 g (of which sugars 43 g), **fibre** 4 g

✓✓   calcium

✓   A, B₁, B₂, C, E, potassium

1 First make the pastry. Sift the flour into a large bowl, then rub in the butter and soft cheese until the mixture resembles breadcrumbs. Sprinkle with 1½–2 tbsp of cold water and mix in using a round-bladed knife, to form a soft dough. Gather the dough into a smooth ball, then wrap in cling film and chill for at least 30 minutes while you make the filling.

2 Preheat the oven to 200°C (400°F, gas mark 6). Peel and thickly slice the apples. Put the sugar and lemon juice in a medium-sized saucepan and heat, stirring, to dissolve the sugar. Add the apples, then cover and cook over a low heat for 8–10 minutes, stirring occasionally, until the apples are just starting to soften but not breaking up.

3 With a draining spoon transfer the apples to a 23 cm (9 in) cake tin (not with a loose bottom) or a pie dish. Stir the sultanas, mixed spice and lemon zest into the juice left in the saucepan and simmer for 2–3 minutes. Pour this mixture over the apples. Set aside to cool slightly.

4 Roll out the pastry dough thinly on a lightly floured surface to a round about 25 cm (10 in). Carefully lay the pastry round over the apple filling, tucking the edges down inside the tin. Bake for 20 minutes or until the pastry is golden.

5 Leave the tart to cool in the tin for 5–10 minutes, then carefully turn out upside-down onto a plate with a rim. Stir together the yogurt, honey and lemon zest, and serve with the tart.

Some more ideas

• Make the pastry dough and the filling a day ahead, then assemble the tart and bake just before serving.

• Instead of lemon zest, use grated orange zest in the fruit filling and yogurt.

• For a pear and walnut tart, use Conference or Comice pears instead of apples, and add 30 g (1 oz) chopped pecans or walnuts with the sultanas and lemon zest (omit the mixed spice).

Plus points

• Sultanas are small white seedless grapes that have been dried. As most of the water is removed in the process, sultanas are a much more concentrated source of sugars, vitamins and minerals than the original grapes.

• Yogurt is usually recommended for the contribution it can make to calcium intake, but it is also a useful source of vitamin B₂, which plays a part in releasing energy from food.

sweet pies and tarts

Apricot flapjack tart

Make the most of aromatic, golden apricots when they're in season by using them in this attractive tart. It has a sweet orange shortcrust base and is topped with a crumbled flapjack-style mixture of oats, sultanas, hazelnuts and seeds. Serve slightly warm for dessert or with morning coffee or afternoon tea.

Serves 6

1 quantity Orange sweet shortcrust pastry (see Some more ideas, page 22), chilled for 30 minutes

Apricot filling

500 g (1 lb 2 oz) fresh ripe apricots, stoned and quartered

3 tbsp orange juice

½ tsp ground mixed spice

1 tbsp clear honey

Flapjack topping

45 g (1½ oz) porridge oats

15 g (½ oz) sultanas

15 g (½ oz) hazelnuts, chopped

1 tbsp sunflower seeds

1 tsp sesame seeds

1 tbsp clear honey

1 tbsp fresh orange juice

Preparation time: 35–40 minutes (including making the pastry), plus cooling and 30 minutes chilling

Cooking time: 30 minutes

Each serving provides ⓥ

kcal 278, **protein** 5 g, **fat** 13 g (of which saturated fat 6 g), **carbohydrate** 38 g (of which sugars 18 g), **fibre** 3 g

✓✓	A
✓	B₁, C, E, copper, iron, potassium

1 To make the filling, place the apricots in a heavy-based saucepan with the orange juice and mixed spice. Bring to the boil, then cover tightly and cook on a low heat for 20–25 minutes, stirring occasionally, until the mixture is thick. Allow to cool, then stir in the honey.

2 Preheat the oven to 190°C (375°F, gas mark 5). Roll out the pastry dough thinly on a lightly floured surface and use to line a 23 cm (9 in) loose-bottomed, non-stick flan tin. Prick the bottom of the pastry case.

3 Bake the tart case 'blind' (see page 19) for 10 minutes, then remove the beans and paper. Bake for a further 5 minutes. Remove from the oven and set aside. Reduce the oven temperature to 180°C (350°F, gas mark 4).

4 To make the topping, mix together the oats, sultanas, hazelnuts, sunflower seeds and sesame seeds. Stir the honey with the orange juice, then stir into the oat mixture.

5 Spread the cooled apricot filling evenly in the tart case. Spoon the oat mixture over the top and press it down lightly. Bake for 12–15 minutes or until the flapjack topping is pale golden. Serve warm.

Some more ideas

• If fresh apricots are not in season, replace them with 2 cans of apricots in natural juice, about 410 g each, drained and chopped. Use a little of the drained-off juice to moisten the flapjack topping instead of the orange juice, and sweeten with just 1 tsp honey.

• To make a plum or damson muesli tart, flavour the pastry with lemon zest and juice instead of orange. For the filling, use halved and stoned plums or damsons instead of apricots, and poach with 4 tbsp apple juice and ½ tsp ground star anise. Cool, then stir in the honey. For the topping, mix together 45 g (1½ oz) porridge oats, 1 small dessert apple, peeled and coarsely grated, and 15 g (½ oz) each dried cranberries and flaked almonds. Bake as in the main recipe.

Plus points

• Apricots are a good source of beta-carotene and some of the B vitamins, and also provide some vitamin C.

• Oats are a good source of soluble fibre, which not only helps to reduce high blood cholesterol levels but slows the absorption of glucose in the body, so helping to maintain a steady blood glucose level.

sweet pies and tarts

Tropical filo baskets

Here's a very pretty dessert. Filo pastry is baked in individual muffin tins to make crisp, petal-like cases, and these are filled with a creamy mango purée topped with papaya and pineapple cubes and pomegranate seeds. The filo baskets can be made ahead but are best filled no more than 1 hour before serving.

Makes 6

25 g (scant 1 oz) unsalted butter, melted

3 sheets filo pastry, 30 x 50 cm (12 x 20 in) each, about 90 g (3¼ oz) in total

Tropical fruit filling

1 large mango, peeled and stoned

2 tbsp fromage frais

1 papaya, cubed

1 small pineapple, cubed

seeds from 1 pomegranate

finely shredded zest of 1 lime

Preparation and cooking time: 40 minutes

Each serving provides Ⓥ

kcal 189, **protein** 4 g, **fat** 5 g (of which saturated fat 3 g), **carbohydrate** 34 g (of which sugars 25 g), **fibre** 5 g

✓✓✓	A, C
✓	B₆, copper, potassium

1 Preheat the oven to 190°C (375°F, gas mark 5). Lightly grease 6 non-stick muffin tins, 7.5 cm (3 in) across and 3 cm (1¼ in) deep, with a little of the melted butter.

2 Lay the filo sheets out on the work surface, one on top of the other. Cut the stack into 12.5 cm (5 in) squares, trimming off the excess pastry. You will have 24 squares.

3 Line each muffin tin with a filo square and brush very lightly with melted butter. Place another square on top, with the corners offset, and brush with butter. Continue layering the filo squares in this way, using 4 for each tin. Bake the filo baskets for 6 minutes or until golden. Leave to cool.

4 For the filling, purée the mango flesh with the fromage frais in a blender or food processor.

5 Shortly before serving, spoon the mango purée into the filo baskets. Top with the papaya and pineapple, and scatter over the pomegranate seeds and lime zest.

Some more ideas

• Instead of pomegranate, scatter over the pulpy seeds of 2 passion fruit.

• Top the mango purée with other fruits such as strawberries, kiwi fruit, peaches or blueberries – whatever is in season and looks pretty.

• Make an apricot and nectarine filo basket. Cut 5 sheets of filo pastry, about 150 g (5½ oz) in total, in half widthways, then trim to make ten 25 cm (10 in) squares. Use the squares to line a lightly buttered moule à manqué tin (a round cake tin with sloping sides) or an 18 cm (7 in) springform tin, arranging the squares and brushing with melted butter as in the main recipe. Bake this large basket for 8–10 minutes or until golden. For the filling, gently cook 250 g (8½ oz) ready-to-eat dried apricots in 150 ml (5 fl oz) orange juice with 2 tbsp brandy (optional) for 20 minutes or until softened. Purée until smooth. Just before serving, spoon the apricot purée into the basket and top with 4 sliced nectarines. Scatter over 15 g (½ oz) roughly chopped pistachios and dust lightly with sifted icing sugar.

Plus points

• Papaya is a useful source of vitamin A, derived from its beta-carotene content. It also provides good amounts of vitamin C plus calcium, iron and zinc.

• Pomegranate seeds are deliciously sweet-tart and crunchy. They make a contribution of vitamin C and fibre to this pudding.

Lemon banana tart

A crisp, sweet shortcrust pastry case is filled with a layer of strawberry conserve and thickly sliced bananas, then topped with a light but luscious lemon and fromage frais mixture that sets as it bakes. No sugar is needed in the filling as the bananas, fruit conserve and lemon curd provide lots of sweetness.

Serves 8

1 quantity Sweet shortcrust pastry, with the finely grated zest of 1 lemon added (see page 22), chilled for 30 minutes

Filling

4 tbsp strawberry conserve

3 firm bananas

5 tbsp lemon curd

250 g (8½ oz) fromage frais

2 eggs, lightly beaten

strawberries to decorate (optional)

Preparation time: 45–50 minutes (including making the pastry), plus 30 minutes chilling

Cooking time: 30–35 minutes

Each serving provides Ⓥ

kcal 266, **protein** 6 g, **fat** 11 g (of which saturated fat 6 g), **carbohydrate** 37 g (of which sugars 22 g), **fibre** 1 g

✓✓	B_{12}
✓	A, B_2, copper, zinc

1 Preheat the oven to 200°C (400°F, gas mark 6) and put a baking sheet in to heat.

2 Roll out the pastry dough thinly and use to line a 23.5 cm (9½ in) shallow, fluted, loose-bottomed flan tin. Prick the bottom of the tart case. Bake 'blind' (see page 19) for 10 minutes, then remove the paper and beans. Bake for a further 5 minutes. Remove from the oven. Reduce the temperature to 180°C (350°F, gas mark 4).

3 Spread the conserve over the bottom of the warm tart case. Slice the bananas, then arrange evenly over the top. Blend the lemon curd with a little of the fromage frais, then stir in the remainder, together with the beaten eggs. Pour over the bananas and spread out evenly.

4 Bake the tart for 30–35 minutes or until the filling is set and lightly browned. Leave in the tin on a wire rack to cool to room temperature before serving.

Some more ideas

• For a chocolate pastry case, make the pastry substituting 25 g (scant 1 oz) sifted cocoa powder for the same amount of flour, and leave out the lemon zest.

• For a ginger and honey banana tart, flavour the pastry with orange rather than lemon zest.

While the tart case is baking 'blind', gently heat 300 ml (10 fl oz) semi-skimmed milk with a 1 cm (½ in) piece of fresh root ginger, roughly chopped, to boiling point. Remove from the heat and infuse for 20 minutes. After baking the tart case, reduce the oven temperature to 160°C (325°F, gas mark 3). Spread 4 tbsp peach or apricot jam over the bottom of the tart case. Arrange 3 sliced bananas over the jam. Blend 1 tsp cornflour with 1 tsp milk in a bowl, then whisk in 2 eggs, 1 egg yolk and 2 tbsp clear honey. Bring the milk back to boiling point and pour onto the egg mixture, whisking constantly. Strain into the pastry case, discarding the pieces of ginger. Bake for 35 minutes or until lightly set. Serve at room temperature.

Plus points

• Bananas have a high potassium content. This mineral is essential for the proper functioning of nerves and muscles in particular, but is also needed by all cells in the body.

• Fromage frais has a wonderfully creamy flavour, but is relatively low in fat. It provides useful amounts of protein, calcium and vitamin B_{12}.

Pear and redcurrant filo lattice

This lovely tart uses sweet and tangy redcurrants with juicy pears for a winning combination. The bright red juice of the currants tints the pears and looks most attractive under the pastry lattice. Although redcurrants only have a short season, they freeze well, so put some in the freezer to make a tart later in the year.

Serves 6

3 sheets filo pastry, 30 x 50 cm (12 x 20 in) each, about 90 g (3¼ oz) in total

20 g (¾ oz) unsalted butter, melted

Filling

2 tbsp redcurrant jelly

1 tsp lemon juice

3 ripe but firm pears, about 170 g (6 oz) each

125 g (4½ oz) redcurrants

45 g (1½ oz) ground almonds

Preparation time: 25 minutes

Cooking time: 15–20 minutes

Each serving provides

kcal 164, **protein** 4 g, **fat** 7 g (of which saturated fat 2 g), **carbohydrate** 22 g (of which sugars 13 g), **fibre** 2 g

✓   C, E, copper

1 Preheat the oven to 200°C (400°F, gas mark 6) and put a baking sheet in to heat. For the filling, place the redcurrant jelly and lemon juice in a small saucepan and heat gently until melted. Remove from the heat.

2 Peel the pears and slice thinly. Add to the jelly glaze and toss gently to coat. Stir in the redcurrants.

3 Lay out 2 sheets of filo on top of each other. (Keep the third sheet covered to prevent it from drying out.) Cut into quarters. Separate the 8 pieces and brush lightly with butter. Use to line a 23 cm (9 in) loose-bottomed, non-stick flan tin, overlapping them slightly, scrunching and tucking in the edges.

4 Sprinkle the ground almonds over the bottom of the tart case. Top with the pear and redcurrant mixture, spreading out the fruit evenly.

5 Cut the remaining sheet of filo crossways in half and brush lightly with butter. Place one half on top of the other, then cut into 10 strips about 2 cm (¾ in) wide, trimming off excess pastry. Twist the doubled strips gently and arrange them in a lattice pattern over the filling, tucking in the ends neatly.

6 Place the tin on the hot baking sheet and bake for 15–20 minutes or until the pastry is crisp and golden brown. Serve warm.

Some more ideas

• Make a pear and raspberry filo lattice by using raspberries instead of redcurrants, and seedless raspberry jam for the glaze rather than redcurrant jelly.

• For a mango and cape gooseberry filo tart, sprinkle the bottom of the tart case with 30 g (1 oz) desiccated coconut. Peel and dice 2 ripe mangoes, about 350 g (12½ oz) each, and mix with 100 g (3½ oz) halved cape gooseberries. Toss the fruit gently with 2 tbsp each of lime juice and light muscovado sugar, then spoon into the pastry case and spread out evenly. Top with the pastry lattice and bake as in the main recipe.

Plus points

• Unlike most fruits, pears contain only a little vitamin C. However in this recipe they are combined with redcurrants, which are a useful source of vitamin C. Pears do offer good amounts of potassium as well as soluble fibre.

• Redcurrants contain more beta-carotene than white currants but less than blackcurrants.

Citrus meringue pie

A modern twist on the well-loved lemon meringue pie, this recipe uses lime and orange as well as lemon in the creamy filling for an exciting citrus flavour. Instead of shortcrust pastry, the case is made with crushed biscuit crumbs held together with egg white, rather than melted butter, to reduce the fat content.

Serves 8

Biscuit crust

150 g (5½ oz) plain biscuits, such as Petit
   Beurre or Abernethy

1 egg white, whisked lightly to loosen

Citrus filling

grated zest and juice of 1 large lemon

grated zest and juice of 1 large lime

juice of 1 large orange

45 g (1½ oz) cornflour

2 large egg yolks

75 g (2½ oz) caster sugar

Meringue topping

3 large egg whites

85 g (3 oz) caster sugar

Preparation and cooking time: 55 minutes,
   plus cooling

Each serving provides Ⓥ

kcal 207, **protein** 4 g, **fat** 5 g (of which
saturated fat 2 g), **carbohydrate** 40 g (of
which sugars 26 g), **fibre** 0.5 g

✓   B$_{12}$

1 Preheat the oven to 180°C (350°F, gas mark 4). To make the crust, put the biscuits in a polythene bag and crush with a rolling pin. Tip into a mixing bowl, add the egg white and stir until the crumbs are all moistened.

2 Spoon the biscuit mixture into a lightly greased, non-stick 21.5 cm (8½ in) sandwich tin (loose-bottomed if you wish). Using the back of the spoon, press the crumbs evenly over the bottom and sides of the tin in a thin layer. Bake for 7–10 minutes or until firm. Leave to cool while making the filling.

3 Combine the lemon and lime zests and juice with the orange juice in a heatproof bowl. Stir in the cornflour to make a smooth paste. Bring 300 ml (10 fl oz) water to the boil in a heavy-based saucepan. Pour the water onto the juice mixture, stirring constantly, then return to the pan. Stir over a moderate heat until it comes to the boil. Reduce the heat and simmer, stirring frequently, for 1 minute or until thick and smooth.

4 Remove the pan from the heat and cool for a minute. Meanwhile, mix together the egg yolks and sugar in a small bowl. Add a little hot citrus mixture, stirring, then stir this into the remaining citrus mixture until thoroughly combined. Pour into the prepared biscuit case.

5 To make the meringue topping, whisk the egg whites until stiff. Gradually whisk in the sugar to make a thick, glossy meringue.

6 Spoon the meringue on top of the citrus filling to cover evenly, swirling it attractively. Bake in the preheated oven for about 15 minutes or until the meringue is golden brown. Leave the pie to cool before serving.

Plus points

• Eggs are one of the few sources of vitamin D. It is found concentrated in the yolk and is not destroyed on cooking. The vitamin A and vitamin B content of eggs is also concentrated in the yolk rather than the white.

• The iron in eggs is not well absorbed on its own, but the vitamin C in both the lemon and lime juice will aid the absorption of this essential mineral in the body.

Some more ideas

• Use crushed ginger nut or digestive biscuits instead of plain ones.

• For an exotic pineapple meringue pie, make the filling using a can of pineapple in fruit juice, about 430 g. Drain the fruit and reserve the juice. Purée the fruit, then stir in 40 g (1¼ oz) cornflour and the grated zest of 1 lime. Make the drained pineapple juice up to 300 ml (10 fl oz) with the juice of the lime and water, then bring to the boil. Pour onto the pineapple purée mixture, stirring well, then return to the pan. Bring back to the boil, then reduce the heat and cook, stirring, until thickened. Cool slightly, then mix with 2 egg yolks and 1 tbsp light muscovado sugar. Pour into the biscuit case. Make the meringue as in the main recipe, but using 45 g (1½ oz) each of caster and light muscovado sugar. Scatter 1 tbsp desiccated coconut over the meringue and bake for 12–15 minutes or until golden brown.

Spiced apple and blueberry pie

Here's the easiest fruit pie you could wish for – a crumbly, half wholemeal shortcrust pastry simply wrapped around a spiced mixture of tangy apples and juicy blueberries, to make a rough parcel with an open top. There's no flan tin to line or pie dish to cover, so it's quick to make and looks sensational too.

Serves 6

Wholemeal shortcrust pastry

75 g (2½ oz) plain white flour

75 g (2½ oz) plain wholemeal flour

1¼ tsp ground mixed spice

75 g (2½ oz) cool unsalted butter, diced

30 g (1 oz) icing sugar, sifted

1 egg yolk

Apple and blueberry filling

550 g (1¼ lb) cooking apples

100 g (3½ oz) blueberries

45 g (1½ oz) light muscovado sugar

1 tsp ground cinnamon

½ tsp freshly grated nutmeg

1 egg white, whisked lightly to loosen

To serve (optional)

vanilla frozen yogurt or Greek-style yogurt

Preparation time: 20 minutes, plus at least
  30 minutes chilling

Cooking time: 30–35 minutes

Each serving provides

kcal 261, **protein 4 g, fat 12 g** (of which saturated fat 7 g), **carbohydrate 38 g** (of which sugars 20 g), **fibre 3 g**

✓   A, C, copper, selenium

1 First make the pastry. Sift the white and wholemeal flours and the spice into a bowl, tipping in the bran left in the sieve. Rub in the butter until the mixture resembles fine breadcrumbs. Stir in the sugar.

2 Mix the egg yolk with 1 tbsp cold water, add to the flour mixture and mix to form a soft dough, adding a few drops more water if needed. Wrap the dough in cling film and chill for at least 30 minutes.

3 Preheat the oven to 190°C (375°F, gas mark 5). Peel and slice the apples, and mix with the blueberries. Stir together the sugar, cinnamon and nutmeg. Reserve 1 tbsp of the mixture, and stir the rest into the fruit.

4 Roll out the pastry dough thinly on a non-stick baking sheet to make a 30 cm (12 in) round. Brush the dough all over with egg white.

5 Pile the fruit mixture in the middle of the pastry round, then draw up the sides over the fruit, but leaving the centre open. Brush the outside of the case with the remaining egg white and sprinkle with the reserved spiced sugar.

6 Bake for 30–35 minutes or until the pastry is golden brown and the apples are tender. Serve warm, with vanilla frozen yogurt or Greek-style yogurt, if liked.

Some more ideas

• For a pastry with more texture, roll out the dough on a surface lightly sprinkled with fine oatmeal.

• Make a deep dish apple and blackberry pie. Replace the blueberries with blackberries, and sprinkle the fruit with the sugar and 1 tsp ground allspice. Place the fruit in a deep 23 cm (9 in) pie dish. Brush the rim with water. Roll out the pastry dough to a round or oval to cover the dish. Lay the dough over the filling and press the edges to the rim to seal. Crimp the edges. Brush the pastry lid with egg white, and sprinkle with ½ tsp caster sugar and a pinch of allspice. Bake in a preheated 190°C (375°F, gas mark 5) oven for 30–35 minutes or until golden brown.

Plus points

• Blueberries are rich in vitamin C and beta-carotene, both powerful antioxidants that help to mop up free radicals before they can do harm to cells in the body.

• Apples provide good amounts of potassium and of soluble fibre in the form of pectin.

• Combining wholemeal flour with white flour increases the fibre content without making the pie crust too heavy.

Sweet Puddings

Satisfying and good for you too

The sweet dish served at the end of a meal is eagerly anticipated, and when it is a healthier version of a classic no one is disappointed. Try a glamorous bread and butter pudding made with brioche and a rum-spiked custard, or a whisked sponge rolled round fresh raspberries and passion fruit. Or what about an old-fashioned charlotte, its crisp, buttery bread case filled with rhubarb and bananas? For autumn, an upside-down pear and blackberry pudding with an orange-scented sponge is a superb way to use the best fruits in season. And, at the end of the year, you could celebrate with a light, fruity Christmas pudding served with a delicate brandy-laced sauce.

Apricot and rum brioche pudding

This glamorous version of bread and butter pudding is based on brioche, the French bread enriched with eggs and butter, and has an egg custard spiked with rum or brandy for a seductive flavour. Sultanas, dried apricots and apricot conserve provide lots of sweetness, so no sugar is needed.

Serves 4

8 medium-sized slices brioche loaf, about 200 g (7 oz) in total

4 tbsp apricot conserve

50 g (1¾ oz) sultanas

100 g (3½ oz) ready-to-eat dried apricots, chopped

2 eggs

450 ml (15 fl oz) semi-skimmed milk

1 tsp pure vanilla extract

1 tbsp dark rum or brandy

Preparation time: 15 minutes, plus 20 minutes soaking

Cooking time: 30–35 minutes

Each serving provides ⓥ

kcal 354, **protein** 13 g, **fat** 9.5 g (of which saturated fat 3.5 g), **carbohydrate** 55.5 g (of which sugars 30 g), **fibre** 3 g

✓✓   B₁₂, calcium, copper, selenium

✓   A, B₁, B₂, niacin, iron, potassium, zinc

1 Spread the brioche slices with the conserve. (If the conserve is a little thick, warm it gently so that it can be spread easily.) Cut the slices in half diagonally or into squares.

2 Arrange the pieces of brioche in a lightly greased 1.2 litre (2 pint) ovenproof dish, scattering the sultanas and chopped dried apricots between the layers.

3 Place the eggs in a mixing bowl. Add the milk, vanilla extract and rum or brandy, and whisk together until well combined. Pour the mixture over the brioche, then gently press the brioche down into the liquid. Leave to soak for 20 minutes.

4 Preheat the oven to 180°C (350°F, gas mark 4). If you like, pull up some of the brioche slices to make a peaked effect. Bake the pudding for 30–35 minutes or until it is just firm to the touch. Serve immediately.

Some more ideas

• If preferred, omit the brandy or rum and add another 1 tsp of vanilla extract.

• For a slightly richer pudding, use whole milk instead of semi-skimmed.

• To make a peach and fruited bread pudding, use 8 slices of a fruit bread instead of the brioche, and spread them with 4 tbsp orange marmalade (with or without shreds of peel).

Replace the sultanas and dried apricots with 115 g (4 oz) chopped, ready-to-eat dried peaches. Instead of vanilla extract, flavour the custard with the grated zest of 1 orange and use 1 tbsp brandy or orange liqueur. Bake as in the main recipe.

Plus points

• Brioche is made from an enriched yeast dough. Like other varieties of bread, it is an excellent source of starchy carbohydrate and contributes to the intake of several vitamins and minerals.

• Dried apricots are not only a useful source of iron, they also contain good amounts of calcium. Regularly using dried apricots in recipes and enjoying them as a snack will help to boost intake of these essential minerals.

• Many of the essential nutrients in milk are concentrated in the non-fat part. Skimmed and semi-skimmed milk therefore contain more of these nutrients than full-fat milk.

Mocha ricotta tiramisu

This delectable version of the popular Italian dessert includes the traditional sponge biscuits soaked in coffee and liqueur for the base, but rather than a rich topping there is a light and creamy mixture of sweetened ricotta cheese and Greek-style yogurt. A sprinkling of grated dark chocolate is the finishing touch.

Serves 4

8 savoiardi or boudoir biscuits (sponge fingers), about 65 g (2¼ oz) in total
1 tsp Continental roast coffee granules
120 ml (4 fl oz) boiling water
2 tbsp coffee liqueur or brandy
1 tsp caster sugar
200 g (7 oz) ricotta cheese
200 g (7 oz) Greek-style yogurt
25 g (scant 1 oz) icing sugar, sifted
1 tsp pure vanilla extract
25 g (scant 1 oz) good plain chocolate (at least 70% cocoa solids), grated, to decorate

Preparation time: 20 minutes, plus at least 30 minutes chilling

1 Break each of the sponge fingers into 3 pieces, then divide evenly among four 240 ml (8 fl oz) glass tumblers or dessert glasses.

2 Place the coffee in a measuring jug and add the boiling water. Add the liqueur or brandy and caster sugar, and stir to dissolve. Pour evenly over the sponge fingers. Leave to soak while you make the topping.

3 Beat the ricotta with the yogurt, icing sugar and vanilla extract until smooth and creamy. Pile on top of the soaked sponge fingers.

4 Sprinkle the top of each dessert with grated chocolate. Cover and chill for at least 30 minutes (but no more than 3–4 hours) before serving.

Some more ideas

• Replace the Greek-style yogurt with fromage frais or vanilla-flavoured low-fat yogurt.
• Instead of grated chocolate, decorate the tops of the desserts by dusting each with ½ tsp of cocoa powder.
• To make an amaretti and raspberry dessert, divide 28 amaretti (or ratafia) biscuits, about 75 g (2½ oz) in total, among 4 glass tumblers or dishes. Add 250 g (8½ oz) raspberries, reserving 12 for decoration. Sprinkle each dessert with 1 tbsp dark rum, brandy or orange liqueur. Make a thick custard using 1½ tbsp custard powder, 2 tbsp caster sugar and

300 ml (10 fl oz) semi-skimmed milk, following the instructions on the label. Flavour with 1 tsp pure vanilla extract. Allow to cool, then blend with 100 g (3½ oz) Greek-style yogurt. Spoon on top of the biscuit and raspberry mixture. Crush 8 more biscuits and scatter the crumbs over the top of the desserts, then decorate with the reserved raspberries. Chill for 30 minutes before serving.

Each serving provides

kcal 253, **protein** 9 g, **fat** 12 g (of which saturated fat 7 g), **carbohydrate** 24 g (of which sugars 20 g), **fibre** 0.5 g

✓✓	A, calcium
✓	B₂, B₁₂, zinc

Plus points

• Ricotta is very much lower in fat and calories than the creamy mascarpone that is traditionally used for this pudding. Adding Greek-style yogurt to the ricotta provides creaminess without loading the fat content.
• Dark chocolate is a good source of copper, a mineral that helps the body to absorb iron. As dark chocolate is also a source of iron, there is a double nutritional benefit to including it in this pudding.

sweet puddings

Spiced flan

A flan can be both a pastry-based tart and a baked custard, like a crème caramel. The flan here is the latter – a feather-light custard based on butternut squash, eggs and soured cream, fragrantly spiced and flavoured with orange. It cuts beautifully into wedges and is delicious served with more soured cream.

Serves 6

1 butternut squash, about 450 g (1 lb)

grated zest and juice of 1 large orange

2 eggs

100 g (3½ oz) light muscovado sugar

1 tsp ground cinnamon

½ tsp ground ginger

¼ tsp freshly grated nutmeg

¼ tsp salt

1 tbsp brandy (optional)

150 ml (5 fl oz) soured cream

To serve

1 tsp icing sugar, sifted

6 tbsp soured cream

Preparation time: 30 minutes, plus at least
  1 hour cooling

Cooking time: 25–30 minutes

1 Peel the squash and cut it into chunks, discarding the seeds. Put into a medium-sized saucepan with the orange juice. Bring to the boil, then lower the heat, cover and cook gently for 20–25 minutes or until tender. Drain, discarding any remaining juice. Purée the squash in a food processor or blender. Preheat the oven to 180°C (350°F, gas mark 4).

2 Lightly beat the eggs in a bowl, then whisk in the orange zest, sugar, cinnamon, ginger, nutmeg, salt, brandy, if using, and soured cream. Add the puréed squash and mix well.

3 Pour the mixture into a 23 cm (9 in) china flan dish or pie dish. Bake for 25–30 minutes or until just set. Loosen the edges with a round-bladed knife, then leave to cool for about 1 hour or, alternatively, until completely cold.

4 Serve slightly warm, or cover and chill before serving. Sprinkle with a light dusting of icing sugar and accompany with extra soured cream.

Another idea

• For a souffléd spiced flan, in step 2, separate the eggs and beat the yolks with the orange zest, sugar, ½ tsp cinnamon, 1 tsp mixed spice, the salt and brandy, if using. Mix with the puréed squash. Whisk the egg whites to soft peaks, then fold into the squash mixture with the soured cream. Pour into a 20–23 cm (8–9 in) ovenproof dish that is 5 cm (2 in) deep. Scatter over 30 g (1 oz) chopped pecan nuts and bake as in the main recipe, until slightly puffy and pale golden. Serve immediately, dusted with icing sugar and with the extra soured cream.

Plus points

• Butternut squash is a good source of the antioxidant beta-carotene as indicated by the bright orange colour of the flesh.

• Soured cream has a lower fat content than double or whipping cream, yet it still adds a rich taste and creamy texture.

• Cinnamon is mentioned frequently in the Old Testament and during the Middle Ages was almost as popular as black pepper. Apart from its culinary use, it appears to have medicinal properties as a nasal decongestant.

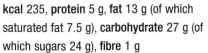

Each serving provides

kcal 235, **protein** 5 g, **fat** 13 g (of which saturated fat 7.5 g), **carbohydrate** 27 g (of which sugars 24 g), **fibre** 1 g

✓✓✓	A
✓✓	C
✓	B₁₂, folate, calcium, potassium

sweet puddings

Raspberry and passion fruit sponge roll

This light, almost fat-free whisked sponge, rolled up round a crushed fresh raspberry and passion fruit filling, makes a very pretty pudding. It's ideal for late summer, when raspberries are particularly sweet. Children will love it. Serve with home-made custard, if you like.

Serves 8

Fruit filling

350 g (12½ oz) fresh raspberries

25 g (scant 1 oz) icing sugar, sifted

4 passion fruit

Whisked sponge

3 large eggs

115 g (4 oz) golden caster sugar

115 g (4 oz) plain flour

1 tbsp tepid water

To decorate

24 fresh raspberries, about 100 g (3½ oz)
  in total

sprigs of fresh mint

To serve (optional)

Real egg custard (see page 29)

Preparation time: 15–20 minutes

Cooking time: 10–12 minutes

1 Set aside half of the raspberries for the filling. Put the rest into a bowl with the icing sugar, and crush lightly with a fork. Cut the passion fruit in half, scoop out the pulp and stir into the crushed raspberries.

2 Preheat the oven to 200°C (400°F, gas mark 6). Grease a 23 x 33 cm (9 x 13 in) Swiss roll tin and line the bottom with baking parchment.

3 Put the eggs and sugar in a large bowl and beat with an electric mixer until very thick and pale, and the mixture leaves a trail on the surface when the beaters are lifted out. (If using a hand whisk or rotary beater, set the bowl over a pan of almost boiling water, making sure the water is not touching the base of the bowl.)

4 Sift half the flour over the whisked mixture and gently fold it in with a large metal spoon. Sift over the remaining flour and fold in together with the tepid water.

5 Pour the mixture into the prepared tin and shake gently so that it spreads evenly into the corners. Bake for 10–12 minutes or until the sponge is well risen and pale golden, and springs back when pressed gently.

6 Turn out onto a sheet of baking parchment that is slightly larger than the sponge. Peel off the lining paper. Trim the crusty edges of the sponge with a sharp knife and make a score mark 2.5 cm (1 in) from one of the shorter edges (this will make the sponge easier to roll up).

7 Spread the crushed raspberry mixture over the hot sponge, leaving a 1 cm (½ in) border all round. Scatter over the reserved raspberries. Carefully roll up the sponge from one of the short edges and place seam side down on a serving plate.

8 Serve warm or cold, cut into slices. Decorate each serving with a few extra raspberries and a sprig of mint. Serve with custard, if liked.

Each serving provides   Ⓥ

kcal 170, **protein** 5.5 g, **fat** 3 g (of which saturated fat 1 g), **carbohydrate** 32.5 g (of which sugars 21.5 g), **fibre** 2 g

✓   A, B₁₂, C, copper

Plus point

• Raspberries not only provide plenty of vitamin C (32 mg per 100 g/3½ oz), they also contain vitamin E, both of which are powerful antioxidants.

Some more ideas

• For a wholemeal sponge roll, use 55 g (2 oz) plain wholemeal flour and 55 g (2 oz) plain white flour.

• Instead of the raspberry and passion fruit filling, spread the warm sponge with 5 tbsp of your favourite fruit conserve, warmed so that it will spread easily.

• Make an apple, strawberry and hazelnut sponge roll. For the filling, put 225 g (8 oz) cooking apples and 225 g (8 oz) dessert apples, both peeled and finely chopped, in a saucepan with 1 tbsp orange juice. Cover and cook gently for 15 minutes, then remove the lid and cook for a further 5–6 minutes, stirring frequently, until most of the fruit juices have

evaporated and the apples are thick and pulpy. Stir in 30 g (1 oz) caster sugar and 170 g (6 oz) sliced small strawberries. For the sponge, replace the flour with a mixture of 55 g (2 oz) each ground hazelnuts and plain flour. Bake, fill and roll up as in the main recipe. When serving, decorate with extra strawberries and sprigs of fresh mint.

Upside-down pear pudding

This comforting pudding is sure to become a family favourite, being perfect for a Sunday lunch on a chilly autumnal day. Pears and blackberries are topped with an orange-scented sponge mixture and baked, then the pudding is turned out upside-down to serve, so the luscious fruit is on top.

Serves 6

55 g (2 oz) golden syrup

3 ripe pears

170 g (6 oz) fresh blackberries

115 g (4 oz) unsalted butter, softened

115 g (4 oz) light muscovado sugar

2 eggs, beaten

170 g (6 oz) self-raising flour

finely grated zest of 1 small orange

2 tbsp semi-skimmed milk, or as needed

To serve (optional)

Greek-style yogurt

Preparation time: 25 minutes

Cooking time: 50–60 minutes

1 Preheat the oven to 180°C (350°F, gas mark 4). Grease a 20 cm (8 in) round, deep cake tin and line the bottom with greaseproof paper.

2 Heat the golden syrup gently in a small pan until it is runny, then pour it over the bottom of the prepared tin. Peel, halve and core the pears. Arrange them, cut side down and in one layer, in the syrup. Scatter over the blackberries.

3 In a mixing bowl, cream together the butter and sugar until pale and fluffy. Gradually add the eggs, beating well after each addition. Fold in the flour, orange zest and milk to give a soft, dropping consistency. Add a little more milk if needed. Spoon the sponge mixture evenly over the fruit in the tin and level the surface.

4 Bake for 50–60 minutes or until risen and golden brown. If the pudding seems to be browning too much towards the end of cooking, cover loosely with foil.

5 Leave to cool in the tin for about 10 minutes, then place an inverted serving plate on top. Turn the tin and plate over, holding them firmly together, so the pudding falls out onto the plate. Serve warm, cut into wedges, with Greek-style yogurt, if liked.

Some more ideas

• For a quick storecupboard pear pudding, use 6 canned pear halves, canned in natural juice, well drained, in place of fresh pears.

• Substitute maple syrup for the golden syrup.

• Try an upside-down pineapple and blueberry pudding, replacing the pears and blackberries with 4 canned pineapple rings, canned in natural juice, well drained, and 170 g (6 oz) fresh blueberries.

• Make an upside-down ginger and plum pudding. Instead of pears and blackberries, arrange 6 halved plums in the syrup. For the sponge mixture use 85 g (3 oz) each of self-raising white flour and self-raising wholemeal flour. Omit the orange zest and add 1½ tsp ground ginger and 3–4 pieces preserved stem ginger in syrup, finely chopped.

Each serving provides

kcal 401, **protein** 6 g, **fat** 18 g (of which saturated fat 11 g), **carbohydrate** 58 g (of which sugars 37 g), **fibre** 3.5 g

✓✓	A
✓	B₁₂, C, E, calcium, copper, iron

Plus points

• Blackberries are high in fibre and vitamin C. They are also one of the richest fruit sources of vitamin E.

• Golden syrup is derived from molasses. It is predominantly made up of the sugars glucose, sucrose and fructose, but because it contains more water and less glucose than table sugar it is not as sweet.

sweet puddings

138

Fragrant gooseberry crumble

Crumbles are always a family favourite and gooseberries are one of the best fruit choices, as their slight tartness partners particularly well with a sweet crumble topping. Here, the flavour of the gooseberries is enhanced with fragrant elderflower cordial and fresh mint, and the crumble topping has oats, hazelnuts and wheatgerm added.

Serves 6

1 kg (2¼ lb) gooseberries, topped and tailed

2 sprigs of fresh mint

2 tbsp elderflower cordial

50 g (1¾ oz) caster sugar, or to taste

Crumble topping

55 g (2 oz) plain white flour

30 g (1 oz) plain wholemeal flour

55 g (2 oz) cool unsalted butter, diced

55 g (2 oz) light soft brown sugar

30 g (1 oz) jumbo oats

30 g (1 oz) hazelnuts, chopped

2 tbsp wheatgerm

To serve (optional)

Real egg custard (see page 29)

Preparation time: 25 minutes

Cooking time: 20–25 minutes

Each serving provides

kcal 275, **protein** 5 g, **fat** 12 g (of which saturated fat 5 g), **carbohydrate** 39 g (of which sugars 25 g), **fibre** 6 g

✓✓	C, E
✓	A, B₁, calcium, copper, iron, potassium, zinc

1 Preheat the oven to 200°C (400°F, gas mark 6). Put the gooseberries in a saucepan with the mint sprigs and elderflower cordial. Cover and cook over a very low heat for 8–10 minutes or until the gooseberries start to soften and release their juices.

2 Stir in the caster sugar until it has dissolved, then transfer to a deep 1.7 litre (3 pint) baking dish, discarding the mint sprigs.

3 Sift the white and wholemeal flours into a mixing bowl, tipping in the bran left in the sieve. Rub the butter into the flour until the mixture resembles breadcrumbs. Stir in the sugar, oats, hazelnuts and wheatgerm. Sprinkle over 1 tbsp cold water and mix in to make a rough crumbly mixture. Spoon the topping evenly over the fruit.

4 Bake for 20–25 minutes or until the topping is golden brown and the fruit filling bubbling. Serve hot or warm, with custard, if liked.

Some more ideas

• For a rhubarb and ginger crumble, cut 1 kg (2¼ lb) rhubarb into 2.5 cm (1 in) lengths and place in a wide, shallow saucepan with 4 tbsp ginger syrup from a jar of stem ginger. Cover and cook gently for 5–6 minutes or until the juices run and the rhubarb is just beginning to soften. Lift out the rhubarb with a draining spoon into the baking dish, leaving the juice in the pan. Sprinkle 45 g (1½ oz) light soft brown sugar over the rhubarb. Simmer the juices for 3–4 minutes or until reduced to about 4 tbsp. Drizzle over the rhubarb. Make the crumble topping with the flours and butter, but add 115 g (4 oz) sweetened muesli instead of the sugar, oats, hazelnuts and wheatgerm. Sprinkle over the fruit and bake as in the main recipe.

• To make a cinnamon plum crumble, quarter and stone 1 kg (2¼ lb) ripe plums and toss with 75 g (2½ oz) demerara sugar and 1 tsp ground cinnamon. Use the crumble topping in the main recipe or the muesli variation above.

Plus points

• This crumble has a lower proportion of fat than the traditional recipe; the crumbly texture is achieved by stirring in a little water. The water evaporates during cooking to give a deliciously crunchy texture.

• Gooseberries are an excellent source of vitamin C. Their high acid content protects the vitamin C, so little is lost during cooking.

• Mint has been used since Biblical times to relieve indigestion. Peppermint tea is still a favourite of many to relieve hiccups and nausea.

sweet puddings

Cherry and pistachio rice pots with cherry compote

This is delightful rice pudding, made wonderfully creamy with fromage frais and full of texture and flavour from the addition of dried cherries and pistachio nuts. It's served in individual pots with a fresh cherry compote, which will keep for several days in the fridge. The pudding is equally good served warm or cold.

Serves 4

Rice pudding

45 g (1½ oz) pudding rice

2 tbsp light muscovado sugar

450 ml (15 fl oz) semi-skimmed milk

25 g (scant 1 oz) dried cherries, halved

30 g (1 oz) pistachio nuts, chopped

few drops of pure vanilla extract

250 g (8½ oz) fromage frais

Cherry compote

2 tbsp redcurrant jelly

25 g (scant 1 oz) golden caster sugar

350 g (12½ oz) fresh cherries, stoned

75 ml (2½ fl oz) fruity red wine, such as
  Beaujolais

Preparation and cooking time: 40 minutes, plus
  15 minutes cooling

Each serving provides Ⓥ

kcal 359, **protein** 11 g, **fat** 10.5 g (of which
saturated fat 4 g), **carbohydrate** 56 g (of
which sugars 46 g), **fibre** 1 g

✓✓	B₁₂, calcium
✓	A, B₁, B₂, C, niacin, copper, potassium, zinc

1 Put the rice in a medium-sized saucepan with the sugar and milk. Stir, then bring to the boil. Reduce the heat and simmer for 20–25 minutes, stirring occasionally, until the rice is cooked and the mixture creamy.

2 Remove the pan from the heat and stir in the cherries, pistachio nuts and vanilla extract. Cool for 15 minutes, then stir in the fromage frais. Spoon into four 170 ml (6 fl oz) little pots or ramekins and set aside.

3 To make the compote, put the redcurrant jelly and caster sugar in a frying pan or wide saucepan and heat over a low heat, stirring, until the sugar has dissolved. Add the cherries and cook gently for 3–4 minutes or until the cherry juices start to run. Pour in the wine, bring just to a simmer and simmer for 1–2 minutes or until the cherries are tender. Serve the compote warm or cold with the rice pots.

Another idea

• For cardamom rice with fresh peach or apricot compote, use flaked rice instead of pudding rice, and add the crushed seeds from 3 cardamom pods with the milk and sugar. Simmer for 15 minutes or until the rice mixture is creamy, stirring occasionally. Cool, then stir in the fromage frais, and pour into pots. For the compote, heat 200 ml (7 fl oz) fruity white wine and 30 g (1 oz) golden caster sugar in a frying pan, stirring, until the sugar has dissolved. Add 4 thickly sliced peaches, or 8 halved apricots. Cover and poach gently for 5–8 minutes or until the fruit is starting to soften. Use a draining spoon to transfer the fruit to a bowl. Boil the liquid in the pan for 6–7 minutes to form a thin syrup. Pour over the fruit, and serve warm or cold with the rice puddings.

Plus points

• Though white rice has less dietary fibre than brown rice, some of the starchy carbohydrate in the white rice is resistant to digestion. This undigested starch seems to aid digestion in a similar way to fibre.

• Fromage frais makes an excellent low-fat alternative to cream for enriching puddings such as this one.

sweet puddings

Rhubarb and banana charlotte

This classic English pudding, of fruit baked in a buttery bread case, is often made with apples, but works very well with an unusual combination of rhubarb and bananas instead. The pudding is thought to take its name from Queen Charlotte, the wife of George III, who had a fondness for growing fruits.

Serves 6

500 g (1 lb 2 oz) young pink rhubarb, thickly sliced

2 tbsp caster sugar

½ tsp ground star anise

finely grated zest and juice of 1 orange

2 large, firm bananas

45 g (1½ oz) unsalted butter, melted

11 thin slices white bread, about 330 g (11½ oz) in total

1 tsp demerara sugar

To serve (optional)

Greek-style yogurt or crème fraîche

Preparation time: 25 minutes

Cooking time: 30–35 minutes

1 Preheat the oven to 200°C (400°F, gas mark 6). Put the rhubarb in a saucepan with the caster sugar, star anise, and orange zest and juice. Cover and cook on a low heat, stirring occasionally, for 10–15 minutes or until the rhubarb is tender.

2 Remove the pan from the heat. Peel and slice the bananas, and stir into the rhubarb. Set aside.

3 Brush the inside of a 20 cm (8 in) springform tin with a little of the melted butter. Remove the crusts from the bread and cut into fingers. Brush lightly with a little of the butter.

4 Arrange about two-thirds of the bread fingers, buttered side in, over the bottom and sides of the tin, leaving no gaps. Tip the fruit into the centre, packing it down firmly. Cover with the remaining bread, buttered side down. Press down lightly and brush with the remaining butter.

5 Bake for 30–35 minutes or until golden brown. Cool slightly in the tin, then turn out and sprinkle with the demerara sugar. Serve warm, with Greek-style yogurt or crème fraîche, if you like.

Plus points

• Rhubarb is 94% water and compared with soft fruit and citrus fruit contains very little vitamin C. However, it is a good source of potassium, which functions with sodium to regulate fluid balance in the body.

• Bananas are a carbohydrate-rich food, containing 2–3 times the amount of carbohydrate in fruit such as apples, oranges and pears and about 50% more than grapes. This is why bananas are popular with athletes, who need to maintain muscle stores of glycogen for long-term energy.

• All varieties of breads make a valuable nutritional contribution to the diet – indeed white bread, which is often perceived to be not as 'healthy' as wholemeal, has twice as much calcium as wholemeal bread.

Each serving provides Ⓥ

kcal 254, **protein** 6 g, **fat** 7 g (of which saturated fat 4 g), **carbohydrate** 44 g (of which sugars 17.5 g), **fibre** 2 g

✓✓   selenium

✓   A, B$_1$, C, calcium, copper, potassium

sweet puddings

Some more ideas

- For a change of shape, make the pudding in a 900 g (2 lb) loaf tin instead of a round tin. Bake at the same temperature for the same time as the main recipe.
- To make a plum, pear and blackcurrant charlotte, poach 500 g (1 lb 2 oz) red plums, halved, in 4 tbsp apple juice with 2 tbsp caster sugar and 1 tsp ground cinnamon for about 15 minutes or until just tender. Remove from the heat and add 2 ripe pears, peeled and chopped, and 100 g (3½ oz) blackcurrants. Pour into the bread-lined tin, then finish and bake as in the main recipe. Before serving, sprinkle with 1 tbsp toasted flaked almonds instead of demerara sugar.
- If fresh blackcurrants are not available for the variation above, use canned blackcurrants in natural juice, well drained, and use the blackcurrant juice rather than apple juice for poaching the plums.

Sticky date and walnut pudding

On a chilly winter day, nothing could be more welcoming than a sponge pudding packed with dates and toasted walnuts. This is very easy to make and it has a lovely moist texture achieved by 'steaming' the pudding in a bain-marie in the oven. A tangy pineapple and marmalade sauce makes a perfect accompaniment.

Serves 8

Sponge pudding

170 g (6 oz) dried stoned dates, chopped

3 tbsp semi-skimmed milk

85 g (3 oz) unsalted butter, softened

85 g (3 oz) light muscovado sugar

2 eggs, lightly beaten

115 g (4 oz) self-raising flour

¼ tsp ground cinnamon

½ tsp ground ginger

50 g (1¾ oz) walnuts, toasted and roughly
   chopped

Pineapple and marmalade sauce

1 can pineapple pieces in natural juice,
   about 400 g

1 tsp arrowroot

4 tbsp fine-cut orange marmalade

Preparation time: 25 minutes

Cooking time: about 1 hour

Each serving provides

kcal 343, **protein** 5 g, **fat** 15 g (of which
saturated fat 7 g), **carbohydrate** 51 g (of
which sugars 39 g), **fibre** 2 g

✓   A, B₁₂, calcium, copper, iron

1 Preheat the oven to 180°C (350°F, gas mark 4). Lightly grease a 900 ml (1½ pint) ovenproof pudding basin and line the bottom with a small disc of greaseproof paper.

2 Place the chopped dates in a bowl and pour over 2 tbsp of the milk. Stir to coat, then leave to soak while preparing the sponge mixture.

3 Put the butter, sugar, eggs and remaining 1 tbsp milk in a bowl. Sift over the flour, cinnamon and ginger, and beat with an electric mixer for 2 minutes or until smooth. Fold in the soaked dates and the walnuts.

4 Spoon the mixture into the pudding basin. Set the basin in a roasting tin and pour in enough boiling water to come 1 cm (½ in) up the sides of the basin. Cover the tin and basin with a tent of foil.

5 Bake for about 1 hour or until the pudding is lightly risen and springy to the touch, and a skewer inserted into the middle comes out clean. If not, bake for a further 10 minutes or so.

6 Meanwhile, make the sauce. Drain the pineapple, reserving 150 ml (5 fl oz) of the juice. Finely chop the pineapple pieces. Blend the arrowroot with a little of the juice in a small saucepan, then stir in the rest of the juice. Bring to the boil and simmer for

1 minute or until thickened and clear. Stir the pineapple and marmalade into the sauce and simmer for a further 2–3 minutes, stirring occasionally.

7 Lift the basin out of the tin and turn out the pudding onto a warmed serving plate. Spoon a little of the hot sauce over the top and serve with the rest of the sauce.

Plus points

• Up to 95% of the energy content of dates comes from natural sugars. The fibre content of dates ensures that the glucose obtained from the sugars is released slowly into the blood stream.

• Walnuts have a high unsaturated fat content, particularly as linoleic acid. Some studies have suggested that including a regular, small quantity of walnuts in the diet can help to reduce high blood cholesterol levels and reduce the risk of heart attacks.

• Pineapple canned in natural juice has a total sugar content of 8.5 g per 100 g (3½ oz) compared to 13.2 g for the same weight of pineapple canned in syrup.

Some more ideas

• Use self-raising wholemeal flour rather than white flour. The mixture will need an extra 2 tsp semi-skimmed milk.

• Instead of a pineapple and marmalade sauce, serve the pudding with a pineapple and orange compote. Just mix the pineapple pieces and their juice with 2–3 sliced or segmented oranges.

• To make mini lemon and sultana puddings, soak 85 g (3 oz) sultanas in 1 tbsp lemon juice and 1 tbsp brandy for 1 hour. Lightly grease eight 100 ml (3½ fl oz) deep muffin tins and line the bottoms with greaseproof paper. Make the sponge mixture as in the main recipe, but leave out the dates and walnuts, and instead fold in the soaked sultanas and the finely grated zest of 1 small lemon. Divide the mixture among the tins and bake for 20 minutes. Meanwhile, make a maple, pecan and citrus sauce. Put 120 ml (4 fl oz) maple syrup in a saucepan with 4 tbsp orange juice, 85 g (3 oz) roughly chopped toasted pecan nuts, the segments from 2 oranges and 1 pink grapefruit, and 1 tbsp orange liqueur, if liked. Gently heat until the sauce is just beginning to bubble. Turn out the puddings onto 8 serving plates. Arrange a few extra orange and grapefruit segments around each pudding, then spoon the hot sauce over the tops. Serve straight away.

sweet puddings

Peach and vanilla choux ring

An impressive dessert for a special occasion or buffet table, this ring of light choux pastry is filled with fresh peaches and a fluffy mixture of fromage frais and whipping cream. It's ideal for entertaining because the pastry ring can be baked ahead of time. Serve decorated with raspberries and pretty cape gooseberries.

Serves 6

1 quantity Choux pastry (see page 23)
150 ml (5 fl oz) whipping cream
150 g (5½ oz) fromage frais
1 tsp pure vanilla extract
4 fresh ripe peaches, chopped
1 tbsp icing sugar, sifted
To decorate
125 g (4½ oz) fresh raspberries
6 cape gooseberries

Preparation time: 35 minutes (including making the pastry)
Cooking time: 30–35 minutes

Each serving provides ⓥ
kcal 310, **protein** 7 g, **fat** 21 g (of which saturated fat 13 g), **carbohydrate** 23 g (of which sugars 13 g), **fibre** 2 g

✓✓✓	A
✓✓	B₁₂, C
✓	B₂, calcium, zinc

1 Preheat the oven to 200°C (400°F, gas mark 6). Put the choux pastry into a piping bag fitted with a 1 cm (½ in) plain nozzle. Pipe a ring of choux pastry, 20 cm (8 in) in diameter, onto a non-stick baking sheet. Pipe a second ring inside and touching the first one, then pipe a third ring on top.

2 Bake for 25–30 minutes or until well risen and golden brown. Using a sharp knife, cut the choux ring in half horizontally. Place the top half, cut side up, on another baking sheet. Return both halves to the oven to bake for a further 3 minutes, to dry out the centres. Transfer to a wire rack to cool.

3 In a mixing bowl, whip the cream with the fromage frais and vanilla extract until thick. Fold in the chopped peaches.

4 Just before serving, spoon the peach mixture onto the base of the pastry ring, and replace the top of the ring. Place the filled choux ring on a serving plate. Dust with the icing sugar and decorate with the raspberries and cape gooseberries.

Some more ideas

• Use 500 g (1 lb 2 oz) mixed strawberries and raspberries in place of peaches.

• Instead of vanilla, flavour the cream mixture with the finely grated zest of 1 lemon or 1 small orange, or 1 tsp ground cinnamon or ginger, or a piece of preserved stem ginger, drained of syrup and finely chopped.

• Sprinkle the filling with 30 g (1 oz) toasted flaked almonds before replacing the top of the pastry ring.

• For a lower fat filling, use 250 g (8½ oz) fromage frais and 3–4 tbsp whipping cream.

• Make a coffee and banana choux ring. For the filling, whip the cream with the fromage frais and 1 tbsp coffee-flavoured liqueur, then fold in 4 sliced, firm bananas.

Plus points

• Peaches are an excellent source of vitamin C. A medium-sized peach provides as much as three-quarters of the recommended daily requirement of this vitamin for adults.

• Whipping cream is lower in fat and calories than double cream. When whipped and mixed with fromage frais, it provides a luscious yet healthier alternative to whipped double cream.

Plum cobbler

A cobbler is an old-fashioned pudding made with a light scone topping and plenty of fruit underneath. This version uses plums, but other fruit in season is good too. The scone mixture has some chopped walnuts added for a nice nutty flavour and texture, and is arranged on the fruit in strips to make an attractive lattice top.

Serves 6

800 g (1¾ lb) plums, halved or quartered

grated zest and juice of 1 large orange

1 cinnamon stick

2 tbsp light muscovado sugar

Scone topping

200 g (7 oz) self-raising flour

pinch of salt

1 tsp baking powder

30 g (1 oz) cool unsalted butter, diced

30 g (1 oz) light muscovado sugar

1 tbsp chopped walnuts

100 ml (3½ fl oz) semi-skimmed milk, plus
   1 tbsp milk for brushing

Preparation time: 45 minutes

Cooking time: 25–30 minutes

Each serving provides Ⓥ

kcal 269, **protein** 5 g, **fat** 7 g (of which saturated fat 3 g), **carbohydrate** 50 g (of which sugars 25 g), **fibre** 3 g

✓   A, B₁, C, E, niacin, calcium, copper, iron, potassium

---

1 Preheat the oven to 180°C (350°F, gas mark 4). Place the plums in a 1.2 litre (2 pint) ovenproof dish. Add the orange zest and juice, cinnamon stick and sugar, and mix thoroughly. Gently shake the dish so the fruit settles in an even layer.

2 To make the scone topping, sift the flour, salt and baking powder into a mixing bowl. Rub in the butter until the mixture resembles fine breadcrumbs. Stir in the sugar and chopped walnuts. Make a well in the centre, add the milk and mix to a soft but not sticky dough.

3 Transfer the dough to a lightly floured work surface and knead briefly. Roll out to a rectangle about 1cm (½ in) thick and the length of the ovenproof dish. Using a sharp knife or a pastry wheel, cut into strips about 1.5 cm (¾ in) wide.

4 Dampen the rim of the dish with water, then arrange the strips over the fruit in a lattice pattern, pressing each end of the scone strips onto the rim of the dish and trimming the ends neatly. Brush the lattice with the 1 tbsp extra milk.

5 Bake for 25–30 minutes or until the scone topping is golden and the fruit is tender. Serve hot or warm. Remember to remove the cinnamon stick when serving.

Some more ideas

• Make the cobbler with a mixture of apples and plums or with the traditional blackberry and apples. Other ideas are apples with raspberries, and pears with berries.

• For a strawberry and rhubarb cobbler, replace the plums with 400 g (14 oz) each chopped rhubarb and whole strawberries, and flavour with the orange zest and 2 tbsp redcurrant jelly. Add chopped toasted hazelnuts to the scone topping rather than walnuts. Roll out the dough to an 18 cm (7 in) round that is 1 cm (½ in) thick and cut into rounds using a 3 cm (1¼ in) fluted cutter. Arrange the rounds on top of the fruit, slightly overlapping, brush with milk and bake as in the main recipe.

Plus points

• Plums are a source of both soluble and insoluble dietary fibre. Soluble fibre helps in reducing high levels of blood cholesterol, whereas insoluble fibre has an important role in preventing constipation.

• Using both the zest and juice of oranges boosts the fibre and vitamin C content. Phytochemicals, which have antioxidant properties, are also present in the skin and therefore included when the zest is used.

sweet puddings

Prune and apple soufflé

There's no need to be nervous about making a soufflé, as it isn't at all difficult. It just needs to be served hot, straight from the oven, while it is impressively puffed up and is light-as-air to eat. This soufflé is flavoured with prunes cooked in apple juice, both naturally sweet, so the mixture needs no sugar to sweeten it.

Serves 4

125 g (4½ oz) ready-to-eat stoned prunes
120 ml (4 fl oz) apple juice
3 large eggs, separated
2 tbsp double cream
2 tsp icing sugar, sifted

Preparation time: 20 minutes, plus at least
    2 hours soaking
Cooking time: 20 minutes

1 Put the prunes in a small saucepan with the apple juice. Cover and leave to soak for at least 2 hours, or overnight if more convenient.

2 Heat the prunes until they start to simmer, then simmer gently for about 5 minutes or until very tender. Purée in the pan with a hand-held blender, or in a blender or food processor.

3 Preheat the oven to 200°C (400°F, gas mark 6), and put a baking sheet in to heat. Lightly grease a 1 litre (1¾ pint) soufflé dish that is 15 cm (6 in) in diameter.

4 In a mixing bowl, lightly whisk together the egg yolks and cream, then stir in the prune purée.

5 In another bowl, clean and grease-free, whisk the egg whites until stiff. Stir 2 tbsp of the egg whites into the prune mixture to loosen it, then carefully fold in the rest with a large metal spoon.

6 Pour the mixture into the soufflé dish. Set on the hot baking sheet and bake for 20 minutes or until the soufflé is risen and just slightly wobbly when very gently shaken. Quickly dust the top with the icing sugar, then serve immediately.

Some more ideas

• For a mango and orange soufflé, replace the prunes with dried mangoes, and simmer in orange juice with 1 tbsp clear honey instead of apple juice.

• To make individual banana and rum soufflés, mash 2 medium-sized ripe bananas until smooth, then stir in 2 tbsp dark rum. Use this instead of the prune purée. Divide the mixture among 6 lightly greased 150 ml (5 fl oz) ramekin dishes. Place on the hot baking sheet and bake for 15 minutes. Dust with icing sugar and serve immediately.

Each serving provides Ⓥ

kcal 198, **protein** 7 g, **fat** 12 g (of which saturated fat 6 g), **carbohydrate** 17 g (of which sugars 17 g), **fibre** 2 g

✓✓	A, B$_{12}$
✓	B$_2$, iron, zinc

Plus points

• Prunes provide useful amounts of potassium, iron and vitamin B$_6$. The vitamin C in the apple juice will help the body to absorb the iron in the prunes.

• Although fruit juices like apple have little fibre – unlike the original fruit – they still retain the other nutrients such as good amounts of vitamin C and other antioxidants.

• Eggs are a useful and convenient food, suitable for both sweet and savoury dishes. They are also good for you, boosting the intake of many essential nutrients including protein, vitamins B$_{12}$, A and D, and zinc.

sweet puddings

Very fruity Christmas pudding

Lighter than the traditional pudding, this is packed with fruit, soaked in sherry and orange juice so it's extra juicy. Served with brandy sauce, this Christmas pudding won't leave you feeling uncomfortably full.

Serves 10

85 g (3 oz) currants

85 g (3 oz) raisins

85 g (3 oz) sultanas

85 g (3 oz) dried stoned dates, chopped

85 g (3 oz) dried apricots, chopped

75 g (2½ oz) dried cranberries

grated zest and juice of 1 large orange

3 tbsp sherry or brandy

115 g (4 oz) unsalted butter, softened

115 g (4 oz) dark muscovado sugar

2 eggs, beaten

1 dessert apple, peeled and diced

1 large carrot, finely grated

30 g (1 oz) flaked almonds, toasted

55 g (2 oz) self-raising flour

2 tsp ground mixed spice

100 g (3½ oz) fresh white breadcrumbs

Brandy sauce

6 tbsp cornflour

900 ml (1½ pints) semi-skimmed milk

3 tbsp caster sugar, or to taste

3 tbsp brandy

Preparation time: 45 minutes

Cooking time: 3 hours, plus 1½ hours

1 Place all the dried fruit in a bowl. Add the orange zest and juice and sherry or brandy, and set aside to soak.

2 Grease a 1.4 litre (2½ pint) pudding basin and place a small disc of greaseproof paper on the bottom.

3 Beat together the butter and sugar until light and fluffy, then gradually beat in the eggs. Add the apple, carrot, almonds and soaked fruits, and mix together. Sift in the flour and mixed spice, and add the breadcrumbs.

4 Spoon the mixture into the pudding basin and smooth the top. Lay a doubled sheet of greaseproof paper and then a doubled sheet of foil on top, and fold together to make a pleat in the centre. Smooth the paper and foil down round the basin and tie securely with string under the edge.

5 Steam for 3 hours, topping up with more boiling water when necessary. Remove the basin from the steamer and take off the foil and greaseproof lid. Cover loosely with a tea-towel and leave to cool.

6 When the pudding is completely cold, cover with doubled sheets of fresh greaseproof paper and foil. Keep in a cool, dark place for up to 3 months.

7 On the day of serving, steam for a further 1½ hours. To make the sauce, blend the cornflour with 6 tbsp of the cold milk. Heat the remaining milk until almost boiling, then pour onto the cornflour mixture, stirring. Return to the pan and stir over a moderate heat until thickened. Simmer for a further 1–2 minutes, still stirring. Add the sugar and brandy, then taste for sweetness, adding a little more sugar if liked.

8 Turn out the pudding onto a serving plate. Pour the hot brandy sauce into a sauceboat or jug and serve with the pudding.

Plus point

• This brandy-laced sauce, made with semi-skimmed milk and thickened with cornflour, provides a much lower fat alternative to cream or brandy butter.

Each serving provides

kcal 432, **protein** 8 g, **fat** 14 g (of which saturated fat 8 g), **carbohydrate** 69 g (of which sugars 53 g), **fibre** 3 g

✓✓✓	A
✓✓	calcium, copper
✓	B₁, B₂, B₁₂, C, E, niacin, iron, potassium, selenium, zinc

Some more ideas

• If preferred, replace the sherry or brandy in the pudding with extra orange juice.

• Make 2 smaller puddings, dividing the mixture between two 750 ml (1¼ pint) pudding basins. They still need 3 hours steaming.

• Rather than steaming, the pudding can be reheated in a microwave. Remove the foil and cook on Medium power for about 8 minutes, or following manufacturer's instructions.

• Make a figgy pudding for Christmas. Use 250 g (8½ oz) chopped dried figs instead of the currants, raisins, sultanas, dates, apricots and cranberries. Soak the figs overnight in 3 tbsp dark rum and the grated zest and juice of 1 lemon. In step 3, use 1 peeled and diced pear in place of the carrot, and add 115 g (4 oz) chopped glacé cherries, rinsed of syrup, and 2 pieces of stem ginger, chopped. Omit the mixed spice. Serve the pudding with a rum and ginger sauce made by flavouring the sweetened white sauce with 3 tbsp ginger syrup (from the jar of stem ginger), 3 tbsp dark rum and the grated zest of 1 lemon in place of the brandy.

A glossary of nutritional terms

Antioxidants These are compounds that help to protect the body's cells against the damaging effects of free radicals. Vitamins C and E, beta-carotene (the plant form of vitamin A) and the mineral selenium, together with many of the phytochemicals found in fruit and vegetables, all act as antioxidants.

Calorie A unit used to measure the energy value of food and the intake and use of energy by the body. The scientific definition of 1 calorie is the amount of heat required to raise the temperature of 1 gram of water by 1 degree Centigrade. This is such a small amount that in this country we tend to use the term kilocalories (abbreviated to *kcal*), which is equivalent to 1000 calories. Energy values can also be measured in kilojoules (kJ): 1 kcal = 4.2 kJ.

A person's energy (calorie) requirement varies depending on his or her age, sex and level of activity. The estimated average daily energy requirements are:

Age (years)	Female (kcal)	Male (kcal)
1–3	1165	1230
4–6	1545	1715
7–10	1740	1970
11–14	1845	2220
15–18	2110	2755
19–49	1940	2550
50–59	1900	2550
60–64	1900	2380
65–74	1900	2330

Carbohydrates These energy-providing substances are present in varying amounts in different foods and are found in three main forms: sugars, starches and non-starch polysaccharides (NSP), usually called fibre.

There are two types of sugars: *intrinsic sugars*, which occur naturally in fruit (fructose) and sweet-tasting vegetables, and *extrinsic sugars*, which include lactose (from milk) and all the non-milk extrinsic sugars (NMEs) – sucrose (table sugar), honey, treacle, molasses and so on. The NMEs, or 'added' sugars, provide only calories, whereas foods containing intrinsic sugars also offer vitamins, minerals and fibre. Added sugars (*simple carbohydrates*) are digested and absorbed rapidly to provide energy very quickly. Starches and fibre (*complex carbohydrates*), on the other hand, break down more slowly to offer a longer-term energy source (see also Glycaemic Index). Starchy carbohydrates are found in bread, pasta, rice, wholegrain and breakfast cereals, and potatoes and other starchy vegetables such as parsnips, sweet potatoes and yams.

Healthy eating guidelines recommend that at least half of our daily energy (calories) should come from carbohydrates, and that most of this should be from complex carbohydrates. No more than 11% of our total calorie intake should come from 'added' sugars. For an average woman aged 19–49 years, this would mean a total carbohydrate intake of 259 g per day, of which 202 g should be from starch and intrinsic sugars and no more than 57 g from added sugars. For a man of the same age, total carbohydrates each day should be about 340 g (265 g from starch and intrinsic sugars and 75 g from added sugars).

See also Fibre and Glycogen.

Cholesterol There are two types of cholesterol – the soft waxy substance called blood cholesterol, which is an integral part of human cell membranes, and dietary cholesterol, which is contained in food. *Blood cholesterol* is important in the formation of some hormones and it aids digestion. High blood cholesterol levels are known to be an important risk factor for coronary heart disease, but most of the cholesterol in our blood is made by the liver – only about 25% comes from cholesterol in food. So while it would seem that the amount of cholesterol-rich foods in the diet would have a direct effect on blood cholesterol levels, in fact the best way to reduce blood cholesterol is to eat less saturated fat and to increase intake of foods containing soluble fibre.

Fat Although a small amount of fat is essential for good health, most people consume far too much. Healthy eating guidelines recommend that no more than 33% of our daily energy intake (calories) should come from fat. Each gram of fat contains 9 kcal, more than twice as many calories as carbohydrate or protein, so for a woman aged 19–49 years this means a daily maximum of 71 g fat, and for a man in the same age range 93.5 g fat.

Fats can be divided into 3 main groups: saturated, monounsaturated and polyunsaturated, depending on the chemical structure of the fatty acids they contain. *Saturated fatty acids* are found mainly in animal fats such as butter and other dairy products and in fatty meat. A high intake of saturated fat is known to be a risk factor for coronary heart disease and certain types of cancer. Current guidelines are that no more than 10% of our daily calories should come from saturated fats, which is about 21.5 g for an adult woman and 28.5 g for a man.

Where saturated fats tend to be solid at room temperature, the *unsaturated fatty acids* –

monounsaturated and polyunsaturated – tend to be liquid. *Monounsaturated fats* are found predominantly in olive oil, groundnut (peanut) oil, rapeseed oil and avocados. Foods high in *polyunsaturates* include most vegetable oils – the exceptions are palm oil and coconut oil, both of which are saturated.

Both saturated and monounsaturated fatty acids can be made by the body, but certain polyunsaturated fatty acids – known as *essential fatty acids* – must be supplied by food. There are 2 'families' of these essential fatty acids: *omega-6*, derived from linoleic acid, and *omega-3*, from linolenic acid. The main food sources of the omega-6 family are vegetable oils such as olive and sunflower; omega-3 fatty acids are provided by oily fish, nuts, and vegetable oils such as soya and rapeseed.

When vegetable oils are hydrogenated (hardened) to make margarine and reduced-fat spreads, their unsaturated fatty acids can be changed into trans fatty acids, or '*trans fats*'. These artificially produced trans fats are believed to act in the same way as saturated fats within the body – with the same risks to health. Current healthy eating guidelines suggest that no more than 2% of our daily calories should come from trans fats, which is about 4.3 g for an adult woman and 5.6 g for a man. In thinking about the amount of trans fats you consume, remember that major sources are processed foods such as biscuits, pies, cakes and crisps.

Fibre Technically non-starch polysaccharides (NSP), fibre is the term commonly used to describe several different compounds, such as pectin, hemicellulose, lignin and gums, which are found in the cell walls of all plants. The body cannot digest fibre, nor does it have much nutritional value, but it plays an important role in helping us to stay healthy.

Fibre can be divided into 2 groups – soluble and insoluble. Both types are provided by most plant foods, but some foods are particularly good sources of one type or the other. *Soluble fibre* (in oats, pulses, fruit and vegetables) can help to reduce high blood cholesterol levels and to control blood sugar levels by slowing down the absorption of sugar. *Insoluble fibre* (in wholegrain cereals, pulses, fruit and vegetables) increases stool bulk and speeds the passage of waste material through the body. In this way it helps to prevent constipation, haemorrhoids and diverticular disease, and may protect against bowel cancer.

Our current intake of fibre is around 12 g a day. Healthy eating guidelines suggest that we need to increase this amount to 18 g a day.

Free radicals These highly reactive molecules can cause damage to cell walls and DNA (the genetic material found within cells). They are believed to be involved in the development of heart disease, some cancers and premature ageing. Free radicals are produced naturally by the body in the course of everyday life, but certain factors, such as cigarette smoke, pollution and over-exposure to sunlight, can accelerate their production.

Gluten A protein found in wheat and, to a lesser degree, in rye, barley and oats, but not in corn (maize) or rice. People with *coeliac disease* have a sensitivity to gluten and need to eliminate all gluten-containing foods, such as bread, pasta, cakes and biscuits, from their diet.

Glycaemic Index (GI) This is used to measure the rate at which carbohydrate foods are digested and converted into sugar (glucose) to raise blood sugar levels and provide energy. Foods with a high GI are quickly broken down and offer an immediate energy fix, while those with a lower GI are absorbed more slowly, making you feel full for longer and helping to keep blood sugar levels constant. High-GI foods include table sugar, honey, mashed potatoes and watermelon. Low-GI foods include pulses, wholewheat cereals, apples, cherries, dried apricots, pasta and oats.

Glycogen This is one of the 2 forms in which energy from carbohydrates is made available for use by the body (the other is *glucose*). Whereas glucose is converted quickly from carbohydrates and made available in the blood for a fast energy fix, glycogen is stored in the liver and muscles to fuel longer-term energy needs. When the body has used up its immediate supply of glucose, the stored glycogen is broken down into glucose to continue supplying energy.

Minerals These inorganic substances perform a wide range of vital functions in the body. The *macrominerals* – calcium, chloride, magnesium, potassium, phosphorus and sodium – are needed in relatively large quantities, whereas much smaller amounts are required of the remainder, called *microminerals*. Some microminerals (selenium, magnesium and iodine, for example) are needed in such tiny amounts that they are known as *'trace elements'*.

There are important differences in the body's ability to absorb minerals from different foods, and this can be affected by the presence of other substances. For example, oxalic acid, present in spinach, interferes with the absorption of much of the iron and calcium spinach contains.
• *Calcium* is essential for the development of strong bones and teeth. It also plays an important role in blood clotting. Good sources include dairy products, canned fish (eaten with their bones) and dark green, leafy vegetables.
• *Chloride* helps to maintain the body's fluid balance. The main source in the diet is table salt.
• *Chromium* is important in the regulation of blood sugar levels, as well as levels of fat and cholesterol in the blood. Good dietary sources include red meat, liver, eggs, seafood, cheese and wholegrain cereals.

• *Copper*, component of many enzymes, is needed for bone growth and the formation of connective tissue. It helps the body to absorb iron from food. Good sources include offal, shellfish, mushrooms, cocoa, nuts and seeds.
• *Iodine* is an important component of the thyroid hormones, which govern the rate and efficiency at which food is converted into energy. Good sources include seafood, seaweed and vegetables (depending on the iodine content of the soil in which they are grown).
• *Iron* is an essential component of haemoglobin, the pigment in red blood cells that carries oxygen around the body. Good sources are offal, red meat, dried apricots and prunes, and iron-fortified breakfast cereals.
• *Magnesium* is important for healthy bones, the release of energy from food, and nerve and muscle function. Good sources include wholegrain cereals, peas and other green vegetables, pulses, dried fruit and nuts.
• *Manganese* is a vital component of several enzymes that are involved in energy production and many other functions. Good dietary sources include nuts, cereals, brown rice, pulses and wholemeal bread.
• *Molybdenum* is an essential component of several enzymes, including those involved in the production of DNA. Good sources are offal, yeast, pulses, wholegrain cereals and green leafy vegetables.
• *Phosphorus* is important for healthy bones and teeth and for the release of energy from foods. It is found in most foods. Particularly good sources include dairy products, red meat, poultry, fish and eggs.
• *Potassium*, along with sodium, is important in maintaining fluid balance and regulating blood pressure, and is essential for the transmission of nerve impulses. Good sources include fruit, especially bananas and citrus fruits, nuts, seeds, potatoes and pulses.
• *Selenium* is a powerful antioxidant that protects cells against damage by free radicals. Good dietary sources are meat, fish, dairy foods, brazil nuts, avocados and lentils.
• *Sodium* works with potassium to regulate fluid balance, and is essential for nerve and muscle function. Only a little sodium is needed – we tend to get too much in our diet. The main source in the diet is table salt, as well as salty processed foods and ready-prepared foods.
• *Sulphur* is a component of 2 essential amino acids. Protein foods are the main source.
• *Zinc* is vital for normal growth, as well as reproduction and immunity. Good dietary sources include oysters, red meat, peanuts and sunflower seeds.

Phytochemicals These biologically active compounds, found in most plant foods, are believed to be beneficial in disease prevention. There are literally thousands of different phytochemicals, amongst which are the following:

• *Allicin*, a phytochemical found in garlic, onions, leeks, chives and shallots, is believed to help lower high blood cholesterol levels and stimulate the immune system.
• *Bioflavonoids*, of which there are at least 6000, are found mainly in fruit and sweet-tasting vegetables. Different bioflavonoids have different roles – some are antioxidants, while others act as anti-disease agents. A sub-group of these phytochemicals, called *flavonols*, includes the antioxidant *quercetin*, which is believed to reduce the risk of heart disease and help to protect against cataracts. Quercetin is found in tea, red wine, grapes and broad beans.
• *Carotenoids*, the best known of which are *beta-carotene* and *lycopene*, are powerful antioxidants thought to help protect us against certain types of cancer. Highly coloured fruits and vegetables, such as blackcurrants, mangoes, tomatoes, carrots, sweet potatoes, pumpkin and dark green, leafy vegetables, are excellent sources of carotenoids.
• *Coumarins* are believed to help protect against cancer by inhibiting the formation of tumours. Oranges are a rich source.
• *Glucosinolates*, found mainly in cruciferous vegetables, particularly broccoli, Brussels sprouts, cabbage, kale and cauliflower, are believed to have strong anti-cancer effects. *Sulphoraphane* is one of the powerful cancer-fighting substances produced by glucosinolates.
• *Phytoestrogens* have a chemical structure similar to the female hormone oestrogen, and they are believed to help protect against hormone-related cancers such as breast and prostate cancer. One of the types of these phytochemicals, called *isoflavones*, may also help to relieve symptoms associated with the menopause. Soya beans and chickpeas are a particularly rich source of isoflavones.

Protein This nutrient, necessary for growth and development, for maintenance and repair of cells, and for the production of enzymes, antibodies and hormones, is essential to keep the body working efficiently. Protein is made up of *amino acids*, which are compounds containing the 4 elements that are necessary for life: carbon, hydrogen, oxygen and nitrogen. We need all of the 20 amino acids commonly found in plant and animal proteins. The human body can make 12 of these, but the remaining 8 – called *essential amino acids* – must be obtained from the food we eat.

Protein comes in a wide variety of foods. Meat, fish, dairy products, eggs and soya beans contain all of the essential amino acids, and are therefore called first-class protein foods. Pulses, nuts, seeds and cereals are also good sources of protein, but do not contain the full range of essential amino acids. In practical terms, this really doesn't matter – as long as you include a variety of different protein foods in your diet, your body will get all the amino acids it needs. It is important, though, to eat protein foods every day because the essential amino acids cannot be stored in the body for later use.

The RNI of protein for women aged 19–49 years is 45 g per day and for men of the same age 55 g. In the UK most people eat more protein than they need, although this isn't normally a problem.

Reference Nutrient Intake (RNI) This denotes the average daily amount of vitamins and minerals thought to be sufficient to meet the nutritional needs of almost all individuals within the population. The figures, published by the Department of Health, vary depending on age, sex and specific nutritional needs such as pregnancy. RNIs are equivalent to what used to be called Recommended Daily Amounts or Allowances (RDA).

RNIs for adults (19–49 years)

Vitamin A	600–700 mcg
Vitamin B_1	0.8 mg for women, 1 mg for men
Vitamin B_2	1.1 mg for women, 1.3 mg for men
Niacin	13 mg for women, 17 mg for men
Vitamin B_6	1.2 mg for women, 1.4 mg for men
Vitamin B_{12}	1.5 mg
Folate	200 mcg (400 mcg for first trimester of pregnancy)
Vitamin C	40 mg
Vitamin E	no recommendation in the UK; the EC RDA is 10 mg, which has been used in all recipe analyses in this book
Calcium	700 mg
Chloride	2500 mg
Copper	1.2 mg
Iodine	140 mcg
Iron	14.8 mg for women, 8.7 mg for men
Magnesium	270–300 mg
Phosphorus	550 mg
Potassium	3500 mg
Selenium	60 mcg for women, 75 mcg for men
Sodium	1600 mg
Zinc	7 mg for women, 9.5 mg for men

Vitamins These are organic compounds that are essential for good health. Although they are required in only small amounts, each one has specific vital functions to perform. Most vitamins cannot be made by the human body, and therefore must be obtained from the diet. The body is capable of storing some vitamins (A, D, E, K and B_{12}), but the rest need to be provided by the diet on a regular basis. A well-balanced diet, containing a wide variety of different foods, is the best way to ensure that you get all the vitamins you need.

Vitamins can be divided into 2 groups: *water-soluble* (B complex and C) and *fat-soluble* (A, D, E and K). Water-soluble vitamins are easily destroyed during processing, storage, and the preparation and cooking of food. The fat-soluble vitamins are less vulnerable to losses during cooking and processing.

• *Vitamin A* (retinol) is essential for healthy vision, eyes, skin and growth. Good sources include dairy products, offal (especially liver), eggs and oily fish. Vitamin A can also be obtained from *beta-carotene*, the pigment found in highly coloured fruit and vegetables. In addition to acting as a source of vitamin A, beta-carotene has an important role to play as an antioxidant in its own right.

• *The B Complex vitamins* have very similar roles to play in nutrition, and many of them occur together in the same foods.
Vitamin B_1 (thiamin) is essential in the release of energy from carbohydrates. Good sources include milk, offal, meat (especially pork), wholegrain and fortified breakfast cereals, nuts and pulses, yeast extract and wheat germ. White flour and bread are fortified with B_1 in the UK.
Vitamin B_2 (riboflavin) is vital for growth, healthy skin and eyes, and the release of energy from food. Good sources include milk, meat, offal, eggs, cheese, fortified breakfast cereals, yeast extract and green leafy vegetables.
Niacin (nicotinic acid), sometimes called vitamin B_3, plays an important role in the release of energy within the cells. Unlike the other B vitamins it can be made by the body from the essential amino acid tryptophan. Good sources include meat, offal, fish, fortified breakfast cereals and pulses. White flour and bread are fortified with niacin in the UK.
Pantothenic acid, sometimes called vitamin B_5, is involved in a number of metabolic reactions, including energy production. This vitamin is present in most foods; notable exceptions are fat, oil and sugar. Good sources include liver, kidneys, yeast, egg yolks, fish roe, wheat germ, nuts, pulses and fresh vegetables.
Vitamin B_6 (pyridoxine) helps the body to utilise protein and contributes to the formation of haemoglobin for red blood cells. B_6 is found in a wide range of foods including meat, liver, fish, eggs, wholegrain cereals, some vegetables, pulses, brown rice, nuts and yeast extract.
Vitamin B_{12} (cyanocobalamin) is vital for growth, the formation of red blood cells and maintenance of a healthy nervous system. B_{12} is unique in that it is principally found in foods of animal origin. Vegetarians who eat dairy products will get enough, but vegans need to ensure they include food fortified with B_{12} in their diet. Good sources of B_{12} include liver, kidneys, oily fish, meat, cheese, eggs and milk.
Folate (folic acid) is involved in the manufacture of amino acids and in the production of red blood cells. Recent research suggests that folate may also help to protect against heart disease. Good sources of folate are green leafy vegetables, liver, pulses, eggs, wholegrain cereal products and fortified breakfast cereals, brewers' yeast, wheatgerm, nuts and fruit, especially grapefruit and oranges.
Biotin is needed for various metabolic reactions and the release of energy from foods. Good sources include liver, oily fish, brewers' yeast, kidneys, egg yolks and brown rice.

• *Vitamin C* (ascorbic acid) is essential for growth and vital for the formation of collagen (a protein needed for healthy bones, teeth, gums, blood capillaries and all connective tissue). It plays an important role in the healing of wounds and fractures, and acts as a powerful antioxidant. Vitamin C is found mainly in fruit and vegetables.

• *Vitamin D* (cholecalciferol) is essential for growth and the absorption of calcium, and thus for the formation of healthy bones. It is also involved in maintaining a healthy nervous system. The amount of vitamin D occurring naturally in foods is small, and it is found in very few foods – good sources are oily fish (and fish liver oil supplements), eggs and liver, as well as breakfast cereals, margarine and full-fat milk that are fortified with vitamin D. Most vitamin D, however, does not come from the diet but is made by the body when the skin is exposed to sunlight.

• *Vitamin E* is not one vitamin, but a number of related compounds called tocopherols that function as antioxidants. Good sources of vitamin E are vegetable oils, polyunsaturated margarines, wheatgerm, sunflower seeds, nuts, oily fish, eggs, wholegrain cereals, avocados and spinach.

• *Vitamin K* is essential for the production of several proteins, including prothombin which is involved in the clotting of blood. It has been found to exist in 3 forms, one of which is obtained from food while the other 2 are made by the bacteria in the intestine. Vitamin K_1, which is the form found in food, is present in broccoli, cabbage, spinach, milk, margarine, vegetable oils, particularly soya oil, cereals, liver, alfalfa and kelp.

Nutritional analyses

The nutritional analysis of each recipe has been carried out using data from *The Composition of Foods* with additional data from food manufacturers where appropriate. Because the level and availability of different nutrients can vary, depending on factors like growing conditions and breed of animal, the figures are intended as an approximate guide only.

The analyses include vitamins A, B_1, B_2, B_6, B_{12}, niacin, folate, C, D and E, and the minerals calcium, copper, iron, potassium, selenium and zinc. Other vitamins and minerals are not included, as deficiencies are rare. Optional ingredients and optional serving suggestions have not been included in the calculations.

Index

Printing and binding:
Printer Industria
Gráfica S.A.,Barcelona
Separations:Colour Systems Ltd,
London
Paper: Condat, France

index